SIMPLE SUPPERS: THE AFTER WORK COOKBOOK

Hugo Arnold has been writing the daily recipe column in the London *Evening Standard* since 1993. Before that he cooked in restaurant kitchens, fed hungry sailors and spent a year hunting spices in India. His main hobby, luckily, he says, remains cooking. This is his first book.

Simple Suppers

THE AFTER WORK COOKBOOK

Hugo Arnold

HEADLINE

First published in 1996
by HEADLINE BOOK PUBLISHING

10 9 8 7 6 5 4 3 2 1

ISBN 0 7472 7809 1

Typeset by
Letterpart Limited, Reigate, Surrey

Printed and bound in Great Britain by
Mackays of Chatham PLC, Chatham, Kent

HEADLINE BOOK PUBLISHING
A division of Hodder Headline PLC
338 Euston Road
London NW1 3BH

ACKNOWLEDGEMENTS

Lindsay Symons, my editor, who diplomatically steered me through the jungle of this, my first book; Alan Brooke, for his enthusiasm; Jacqueline Korn, my agent, for all her support; Alison Thompson, whose recipe testing was unfailingly thorough and helpful; my mother for her suggestions and useful comments on the text; Cara Hobday, who magnificently interpreted the recipes for the photographs; Iain Bagwell, whose camera-work and approach were faultless; and most of all Sue, who has tested, starved, coped with my absences, and given endless and useful advice with her characteristic optimism. Any faults are, of course, mine.

CONTENTS

Introduction

This book is about preparing and enjoying simple food. It is for those who take pleasure from a little well-organised time in the kitchen, who look forward to sitting down and eating good food at the end of the day. It is about using the best available ingredients, not the most exotic, about being efficient, without cutting corners – there are no gimmicks involved in preparing good, simple food.

I want to sit and eat with my family and friends and this is only practical if I cook quickly and simply; food on the table at a reasonable hour gets more marks in my household than some complicated extravagance served up at 10 o'clock. Flavours must be bold, not fussy, ingredients few rather than many, cooking methods fast: for the art of slow simmering you must look elsewhere. Most of the recipes in the book can be on the table well inside an hour, some involve overnight soaking or marinating, but most do not.

Keeping a good table is an old-fashioned phrase, but as relevant today as it ever was. Eating well is the objective and the taste, texture and appearance of the food must reflect that. After all, if a dish looks boring, why would anyone want to eat it? I once worked for a chef whose constant question was, how do you feel about that dish? If the answer wasn't an unqualified 'brilliant', chances were it wasn't right. How you feel about a dish should not be underestimated, whether it's Welsh rabbit (or rarebit) and a glass of beer, or roast monkfish with pancetta, garlic and rosemary and a bottle of Chablis.

These recipes are a collection of the borrowed, stolen, so-called original, adapted and rearranged – for what recipe is truly new? I hesitate to claim the hand of invention, and anyway, once you have cooked a dish in a very real sense it becomes yours. The printed word is a starting point, a guideline, a helping hand through some essential steps; after that, the role as artist, craftsman, scientist is firmly in the hand of the cook. Recipes change as they are passed from one cook to another and most are all the better for that process. My favourite cookery writers are also the ones who have encouraged me to experiment, increased my confidence and helped when I have stepped, a trifle uncertainly, into areas about which I knew little. I hope this book will do the same.

All these recipes have been tested carefully, but not in a laboratory. If your instinct leads you to vary the ingredients or the method, I suggest you follow it. I would. As for quantity, my friends and family say I tend to be over generous, but then I'm a little greedy and I love leftovers. When I say a recipe feeds four, it means four healthy eaters.

With many of the recipes the list of ingredients is quite short, with the main focus concentrating on a few fresh items which can, in most instances, be bought on the day. I know most of us don't shop for food every day, but even shopping for fresh food twice a week is better than loading up your fridge with good ingredients on Saturday, only to watch them slowly deteriorate towards the following Friday. Domestic fridges are at best temporary holding operations; your main depot should always remain the shops.

This approach relies, however, on maintaining a good store cupboard, a description too often misapplied to jars and cans that will, in an emergency, feed you. Keep a rations-supply if you wish, but alongside this you should have some or all of the dried goods listed on pages 6–7, along with a few chilled items. I'm not suggesting you need to go out and buy all of these at once, simply that shopping becomes a much more enjoyable exercise if you can rely on having these things at home.

The contents of a store cupboard are just as important as the list of ingredients in a recipe and they, too, must be fresh (i.e. within their sell-by date) and accessible. Searching madly for some half-remembered packet of couscous at the back of the cupboard bought for that party two years ago is dangerous hunting.

For a nation of shopkeepers, we have become remarkably reluctant about food shopping. Few people seem to enjoy it and yet we are faced with more choice and greater variety than ever before. Supermarkets are playing a leading and powerful role in this, establishing standards which are the envy of many other countries. What is sad is that other traders have been unable or reluctant to rise to the challenge. With few exceptions, street markets are abysmal, selling shoddy produce and complaining if you touch anything. On the other hand, local delis and supermarkets, which most old-fashioned grocers have become, are often helpful, open to suggestion and willing to try new ingredients and products if only we, the customers would talk with them.

If you have a good fishmonger, use him or her. They have a skill and knowledge that the supermarkets, try as they might, can never match. Chat with them as well: their business is selling what you want, so discuss, suggest, encourage. We buy fish in this country that is days old. In Spain, even in towns and villages far from the sea, it is hours old – why? Because they like eating fish and say so. We have somehow lost this power, so the large chains dictate to us what is available and we smile in appreciation. We must relearn the ability to demand – not aggressively, but by persuasion – standards and choice in our food.

We produce some of the best meat and game in the world in these islands but have a butchery tradition that is fast disappearing. A good butcher is the source of much time- and money-saving. Buy a fillet of lamb from him and all you need to do is roast it; buy some pork knuckles and you can feed a multitude on pence rather than pounds. Supermarkets sell prime cuts while butchers buy and must sell whole carcasses. The butcher's off-cuts are the source of cheap and delicious eating.

Keeping cheese in good condition is a complicated, skilled and expensive business – few have the knowledge. If you are lucky enough to have a good cheese supplier, buy small amounts and often: the fridge is a hostile environment and cheese doesn't like wearing cling film.

It can be tempting to buy all your pasta, dried beans, lentils and tinned products from supermarkets, which generally stock a good range. In my experience, however, although you may pay more, a good delicatessen often has superior brands – this is certainly the case with pasta, lentils and some tinned products. At the same time, there are some delicatessens which try to sell products available in the local supermarkets with a ridiculous mark-up. In this case, the supermarket is obviously a better bet.

Buy the best utensils you can afford, and shop around: there is a lot of stylish rubbish about which is best ignored. Knives should see a sharpener before they greet a carrot – every time, not just when you remember. If you buy good knives and keep them sharp you'll save a lot of time and probably your fingers as well – blunt knives cause more accidents than sharp ones because they tend to slip on whatever you are cutting. I have an addiction to wooden spoons and forks – I buy them at every opportunity and can't bear to throw any away – but I'm wary of gadgets. Too often the time saved is spent cleaning all the fiddly bits and I'd rather use my knives and a decent large chopping board. Exceptions would be a mouli, a mandolin and at least three of those cheap metal vegetable peelers shaped like a 'U' with the blade across the top, which means I can get lots of people to help. I used to hesitate about asking people to help – not any more. Not only does everything happen more quickly if they do, but everyone feels involved and part of the preparation.

Organising yourself in the kitchen is one of the major time-saving aspects of cooking. Knowing where everything is and moving logically from one step to the next without hesitation can reduce preparation time substantially. Always try and get some job going that can continue while you are getting on with something else. This may mean potatoes baking in the oven, or it might mean someone else chopping parsley while you make mayonnaise; but the more you get under way, the quicker things will happen. I always put the kettle on automatically and the occasions are rare when I don't end up using it at some point, even if it is just to make a cup of tea.

Desserts are rarely eaten during the week; fruit always is. Cheese is usually available. It is a rare meal where we don't eat salad, preferably with a variety of different leaves. A range of oils and vinegars ring the changes, but there is nothing like raw leaves to cleanse the palate.

Salad is also important for the balance of a meal. Together with the other vegetables, bread, pulses, rice, pasta and fruit, it should make up the bulk of what we eat. An excessive reliance on fat-rich, over processed foods is considered harmful to our long-term health. That we are what we eat is, like so many clichés, true.

Taste, taste and taste again. Fresh herbs add lightness, balance, a freshness of flavour for which there is no substitute. With the exception of oregano and bay leaves, dried herbs taste like dust and I have no hesitation in urging you to hurl them into the bin. Spices are better freshly ground, but above all else, remember they have a relatively short shelf life, whether whole or ground. It may appear extravagant, but every January I ditch all my spices along with my resolutions and start again.

As for salt, Maldon sea salt has no equal in my opinion. If you don't believe me, taste it alongside whatever brand you do use. It has a fresh tang of the sea that is almost sweet. Pepper, which I would have to have on my desert island, must be black and ground as it is used. The volatile oils contained in the seeds have a very short life, and there is simply no point in using the ready ground variety.

I adore olive oil and use it all the time in my cooking, but I think a lot of fuss is made about it. Prices range almost as widely as the labels and bottle shapes. Cook with something neutral and inexpensive – the process of heating destroys most of the subtleties anyway. For dribbling over grilled foods and salads, it must be extra virgin and cold pressed, but don't be swayed by the presentation. There are a lot of indifferent oils dressed up to look like old masters and it's the taste that counts: your taste, that is. It's also worth remembering that Italy is not the only country with olive trees. Greece, France, Portugal and Spain are all producing interesting olive oils; the latter is still the only one to have an appellation control system similar to wine.

Finally, a note on measurements. As a general rule, measurements are meant as a guide, except in the dessert section, where they are exact. A spoon, whether it is a tea, dessert or tablespoon, means lightly heaped. A glass means 175 ml (6 fl oz); a handful is what you can comfortably grasp in your hand; eggs are size two. Use Imperial or metric measurements, but never mix the two.

Store cupboard and chilled items

Pasta (several different shapes)	*Olive oil*
Rice (several different varieties)	*Vinegar*
Beans, both dried and tinned	*Dijon mustard*
Lentils	*Black peppercorns*
Chickpeas, both dried and tinned	*Maldon Sea Salt*
Couscous	*Bottled or tinned tomatoes*
Polenta	*Tinned tuna fish*

Bottled anchovy fillets
Olives
Capers (preferably in salt)
Pine nuts
Dried mushrooms
Strong white bread flour

'00' (pasta) flour
Caster sugar
Parmesan
Pancetta
Butter

Egg Dishes

Crack open a few eggs and supper is never far away: baked, scrambled, fried, poached or boiled, they make a noble instant feast. I still dip soldiers of hot buttered toast into a boiled egg and am reminded of Sunday evening suppers whenever I eat scrambled eggs. Omelettes, always with a glass of wine, celebrate fresh herbs. Poached eggs are a favourite brunch food, except I can never wait for brunch and have them for breakfast instead. Worked into a delicious sauce – hollandaise or bearnaise – and dribbled over some steamed fish or vegetables, they make a grand supper.

Egg production methods are many and varied, almost as varied as the terms used to describe them: class A, size 2, free-range, barn-fresh, farm-fresh. I find the whole business confusing and not a little depressing. I want my egg so the yolk is a natural deep yellow and the white is thick, viscous and gooey. I also want the hens to have a good life, grubbing around for food and being able to chat and argue with their friends.

I have shopped around for my free-range eggs with both good and bad results and I can only advise you to do the same. The confusing general terms on the boxes are often expanded on by the better producers. If you find a good one, stick with them.

SCRAMBLED EGGS WITH FRESH HERBS AND CRISPY PANCETTA

Pancetta is to the Italians what streaky bacon is to us, although it's better. It is exactly the same cut of bacon as streaky, but is cured for about 20 days. One advantage of this is its tendency to go crispy without too much cooking, which is rather the point of this recipe – creamy soft eggs infused with the aroma of fresh herbs and crunchy slices of pancetta. Perfect late-night feasting when speed is necessary.

SERVES 4

25 g (1 oz) butter
6 eggs, lightly beaten
5 tablespoons single cream
salt and pepper

110 g (4 oz) pancetta
1 tablespoon each of chopped parsley,
   chives, basil, chervil and dill

METHOD: Melt the butter in a saucepan, whisk in the eggs and the cream, season with salt and pepper and cook over a moderate heat until the eggs are just set. Meanwhile grill the pancetta under a hot grill until it goes crispy. Stir the herbs into the eggs and serve immediately with the strips of pancetta criss-crossed on top, with lots of hot buttered toast.

SORREL OMELETTE

Driving back to New Delhi one night from a hill station in the Himalayas, I stopped at a roadside café where a Sikh chef, resplendent in the most wonderful turban, was cooking up omelettes. We all chose our respective fillings and he proceeded to make the fluffiest, most succulent omelettes I have ever eaten, more fried soufflé than omelette. To this day, all omelettes are compared against the one I ate that night. The garish neon lights and horrifically loud Indian music, the gentle wafting smell of spices – it all floods back.

Sorrel is making a slow but steady return – not before time – and can usually be found in supermarkets alongside equally small packets of rocket. Buy more of this wonderful leaf and we might see the price fall and quantity rise. It has a natural affinity with eggs, is a delight with fish and gives a bright lemony tang to a salad if used in moderation.

SERVES 2

handful of sorrel leaves   *1 tablespoon crème fraîche*
50 g (2 oz) butter   *4 eggs*
nutmeg   *a little chopped parsley*
salt and pepper

METHOD: Roll the sorrel leaves up like a cigar and with a sharp knife cut into rough strips. Melt the butter in a frying pan and add the sorrel leaves. Cook over a very low heat so the sorrel just wilts. Remove from the heat, add a grating of nutmeg, a seasoning of salt and pepper and the crème fraîche.

Whisk the eggs up lightly and season with salt and pepper. Add a little butter to a clean frying pan, add the eggs and cook the omelette until almost set. Pour in the sorrel mixture, fold over and allow to cook for two minutes before serving with a sprinkling of parsley.

FRITTATA OF COURGETTE WITH LEMON AND PARSLEY

Frittata – in essence a slow-cooked omelette – can, and frequently does, have almost anything in it, including pasta, or whatever leftover vegetable is languishing in the fridge. The secret is to limit the range of items you use. A little bowl of leftover vegetable will work best, maybe with some cheese, as in this recipe, but not with countless other leftovers which will only serve to confuse the various flavours. Whereas an omelette is cooked quickly over a high heat, a frittata slowly sets over a gentle heat and is then finished off under the grill.

SERVES 4–6

450 g (1 lb) courgettes
salt and pepper
6 eggs
3 heaped tablespoons chopped parsley

50 g (2 oz) freshly grated Parmesan
juice and zest of 1 lemon
50 g (2 oz) butter

METHOD: Grate the courgettes on the largest setting of your grater. Sprinkle over two teaspoons of salt, toss well and set aside for 10 minutes. *Very lightly* beat the eggs: you specifically don't want to introduce air bubbles. Add the parsley, a seasoning of salt and pepper, the Parmesan and the juice and zest of the lemon. Rinse the courgettes thoroughly under cold water and squeeze dry in a tea towel.

Heat the butter in a frying pan and gently sauté the courgettes for 10 minutes. Remove and add to the eggs. Return the whole lot to the frying pan, wiped clean and smeared with a little butter, and cook over a low heat until almost set, about 10 minutes. Meanwhile, preheat the grill. When the frittata is almost set, place under the grill for two minutes until lightly browned and serve.

Cold frittata makes a delicious snack if kept in the fridge. Cut into wedges it is a welcome treat when you fall in the door starving after a long day.

GRILLED VEGETABLES WITH
POACHED EGG

Every time I visit Spain I like it more and more. The wildness of the countryside, the passion of the people, their unbridled enthusiasm: it's a heady combination. These characteristics are matched by a cuisine that utilises some of the most wonderful ingredients – Jamon Serrano, the unparalleled chorizo sausage, and olive oil that is some of the best in the world. Piperrada is a Basque dish where vegetables are sautéed in olive oil until soft, then eggs are broken into the mixture to cook in the gentle heat as the dish is carried to the table. My version has the same components, but from there it sails off on its own course: vegetables grilled not fried, and the eggs poached separately. Cut into that yolk, however, and as the golden liquid tumbles down the whole assembly smells and tastes delicious.

SERVES 4

olive oil	*2 red peppers*
2 garlic cloves, peeled and chopped	*2 yellow peppers*
salt and pepper	*white wine vinegar*
4 courgettes	*4 eggs*
1 aubergine	*1 tablespoon finely chopped parsley*

METHOD: Combine 5 tablespoons of olive oil with the chopped garlic and a generous seasoning of salt and pepper. Cut the courgettes and aubergine into 1 cm (½ inch) slices and brush with the oil. Preheat the grill, and brown the vegetables on both sides – if you have a ridged griddle pan, so much the better.

Cut the peppers in half, deseed and grill, skin side up, until black and charred. Transfer to a bowl, cover with cling film and allow to sweat for five minutes. Remove the cling film and when cool, peel. Arrange all the vegetables on 4 plates and keep warm.

Bring a saucepan of salted water to the boil, add a generous dash of vinegar and gently slide in the eggs. Poach for three minutes, remove with a slotted spoon and serve on top of the vegetables. Sprinkle with parsley and serve.

To drink: a chilled dry fino sherry, and don't be afraid of drinking a bottle between four. This is a fantastic wine, full of spicy, nutty aromas and bone dry. It will put you in Spain instantly.

SPINACH HOLLANDAISE WITH RATTE POTATOES

Over the years I have come to the conclusion you can never make enough hollandaise sauce. I have doubled, even trebled the quantity and still there will be somebody who, piece of bread in hand, or potato on the end of a fork, is chasing the last few remaining drops around the bowl.

If you cannot get hold of Ratte potatoes, try one of the other salad varieties, such as Pink Fir Apple or Charlotte. In season, Jersey Royals are hard to beat.

SERVES 4

450 g (1 lb) spinach
12 Ratte potatoes
2–3 tablespoons vinegar
1 tablespoon chopped shallot
4 peppercorns

4 egg yolks
225 g (8 oz) butter
salt and pepper
lemon juice to taste

METHOD: Blanch the spinach in boiling water for 2 minutes, drain, refresh under cold water and pat dry. Arrange in four lightly buttered gratin dishes. Steam or boil the potatoes until cooked, cut in half and scatter on top of the spinach.

Combine the vinegar with an equal quantity of water in a saucepan, add the shallot and peppercorns and simmer over a medium heat until reduced to two tablespoons. Strain the liquid into a bowl, stir in the egg yolks and sit in a saucepan of barely simmering water. Whisk in the butter, one lump at a time, then season with salt and pepper and add lemon juice to taste. Pour over the spinach and potatoes and flash under a preheated grill until the surface browns slightly. Serve with lots of bread.

A lot of the flavour in a potato comes from the skin, so it's best to buy them wrapped in a protective layer of earth. Once you start washing and scrubbing, you begin to remove some of the flavour. Use a cloth and be gentle – the potatoes will thank you for it.

Roast Bacon and Eggs

The full cooked breakfast, as guest houses like to refer to it, may be a treat to eat but it's not much fun if you are the one cooking it. As you stand there bleary-eyed and wishing you were still in bed, the bacon spits, the sausages split and the egg yolks invariably break – and it's no better if you're trying to carry out this operation post pub or late at night when it's all you have in the fridge. This recipe removes all the nasty aspects of this meal to the confines of the oven, which means you too can experience that gentle wafting aroma of cooking bacon instead of a wave of spitting fat.

SERVES 4

vegetable oil for frying
4 sausages
8 slices of bacon

4 eggs
salt and pepper

METHOD: Preheat the oven to gas mark 6/400°F/200°C.

Put one tablespoon of vegetable oil in a roasting tin or metal-handled frying pan. Lightly coat the sausages in the oil, arrange the bacon in a single layer and roast in the oven for 15 minutes, turning once.

Break the eggs on top of the bacon and return to the oven for 5 minutes, or until the eggs are cooked. Season with salt and pepper and serve with plenty of toast and hot tea or coffee.

GRILLED LEEKS WITH ANCHOVY AND CHOPPED-EGG SALAD

The anchovy is an extraordinary fish too often served in every other way but fresh. Salted, canned, smoked, dried and, in South East Asia, turned into fish sauce, it is remarkably distinctive and yet works extremely well with other flavours. Try roasting a leg of lamb with anchovies crisscrossed over the top: the melting flavour of the anchovy perfectly cuts the fattiness of the lamb. If fresh anchovies are unavailable, buy the pale ones sitting spoke-like in a round tub from your Italian delicatessen. The tinned brown salty variety will not do for this recipe.

SERVES 4

8 small leeks	*4 lemons*
salt and pepper	*olive oil*
12 fresh anchovies (or the pale variety	*bunch of parsley*
in oil, available from Italian	*2 hard-boiled eggs*
delicatessens)	

METHOD: Trim the leeks and blanch in boiling salted water for 8 minutes. Drain, refresh under cold water and pat dry.

If using fresh anchovies, with a sharp knife gently cut two slices either side of the anchovy's head and down the belly, as you normally would with any fish. Pull the head down towards the tail and the whole backbone should come away. Wash thoroughly and pat dry. Put the anchovies in a bowl, add the juice of 2 lemons, 2 tablespoons of olive oil and a dessert-spoon of chopped parsley, and allow to marinate in this solution for 20 minutes.

Brush the leeks with olive oil and grill until just slightly charred. (If you have a griddle then use that – it will produce those stylish black lines.) Shell the eggs and chop finely. Sprinkle the egg and the anchovies (or preserved anchovies if using) on top of the leeks, and serve with a drizzle of olive oil, some salt and pepper and a lemon half to squeeze over.

Smoked haddock and scrambled eggs with lumpfish caviar

Much as I adore smoked salmon, it is sometimes in danger of overshadowing the other smoked fish we have – kippers, eel, haddock, cod's roe, all of them equally delicious. The smoking transforms both the flavour and the texture but maintains the inherent qualities of the fish. With the haddock, you still get that deliciously sweet nutty chewiness and the smoke infuses with the eggs. A luxurious supper dish.

SERVES 4

50 g (2 oz) butter
5 tablespoons single cream
225 g (8 oz) smoked haddock
6 eggs, lightly beaten

salt and pepper
1 tablespoon chopped parsley or chives
1 jar black lumpfish caviar

METHOD: Melt the butter in a saucepan, add the cream and the fish, cover and gently simmer for 10 minutes, or until the fish is cooked. Remove the skin from the fish and flake. Pour the cream and butter mixture into a clean saucepan and stir in the eggs over a low heat until almost cooked. Return the fish to the pan and finish cooking. Season to taste, stir in the parsley and spoon on to plates. Add a dollop of the caviar and serve with thin slices of toast.

Anchovies also work well with scrambled eggs, as does smoked salmon, particularly the dark off-cuts which are usually sold more cheaply than the prime cuts.

EGGS EN COCOTTE WITH SMOKED TROUT AND SPINACH SALAD

Smoking fish dramatically alters its taste and texture, providing you with two different flavours from the same source. I'm not too keen on the fresh variety of farmed trout, but its smoked cousin, provided it is from a good supplier, can form the basis of a rather delicious supper dish. Baked eggs were a tea-time treat throughout my childhood, and this recipe is still a favourite for those late evenings when I'm starving but too tired to cook. Together with a pot of Darjeeling tea and some hot toast, it's guaranteed to make me feel human again.

SERVES 6

110 g (4 oz) butter
2 fillets smoked trout
ground mace
salt and pepper
1 dessertspoon chopped parsley

6 eggs
110 ml (4 fl oz) single cream
450 g (1 lb) spinach
toast

METHOD: Preheat the oven to gas mark 4/350°F/180°C.

Cut six discs of greaseproof paper, generously butter and arrange in the base of six well-buttered, size-one ramekins (about 7 cm – 2¾ inches – in diameter). Flake the trout and divide equally among the ramekins. Dust with a little mace, season well with salt and pepper and sprinkle over a little parsley.

Lightly whisk the eggs with the single cream and divide among the ramekins. Bake in the oven for 10–15 minutes, or until the eggs are set. Blanch the spinach in a pan of salted water for 2 minutes, drain and toss with the remaining butter, season well and divide equally on six plates. Ease the edges of the baked eggs with a palette knife, turn on to a towel and then back on to the spinach, so the golden top is uppermost. Serve with plenty of toast.

CRAB AND GINGER SOUFFLÉ

I used to be terrified of crabs as a child, convinced that their sideways swing was just a ploy to lure me in before they switched tactics to a full-frontal attack. Swimming off the beaches in the west of Ireland, the sand would be littered with the corpses of tiny crab-orphans, washed from their hiding places and mercilessly destroyed. My suspicious mind was convinced their parents were out to wreak revenge on my toes. My own revenge has finally come, and it is particularly sweet, crab meat having a succulent richness that is, for me, perfect and superior to lobster any day.

Soufflés are nothing like as difficult as some people make out. They are quick, easy and cheap, but more importantly, they have a sublime taste and texture.

SERVES 6

25 g (1 oz) butter	*2 tablespoons cream*
2 tablespoons plain flour	*1 scant teaspoon freshly grated ginger*
275 ml (½ pint) milk	*4 eggs, separated*
cayenne pepper	*salt and pepper*
225 g (8 oz) cooked crab meat – a	*a little extra butter to grease the*
large crab gives about	*moulds*
450 g (1 lb) of meat	*handful of breadcrumbs*

METHOD: Preheat the oven to gas mark 6/400°F/200°C.

Melt the butter over a moderate heat and stir in the flour. Cook without browning for 5 minutes, whisk in the milk and continue cooking for a further 5 minutes, or until the sauce thickens and is smooth. Add a pinch of cayenne pepper, along with the crab meat, cream, ginger, egg yolks and a generous seasoning of salt and pepper.

Lightly butter six size-two ramekins (about 8 cm – 3¼ inches – in diameter) and dust with the breadcrumbs. Stiffly beat the egg whites and gently fold into the crab mixture. Divide the mixture up among the ramekins and bake for 10–15 minutes, or until risen and set.

Tip: The base mixture can be prepared ahead of time, but needs to be at room temperature when you incorporate the egg whites. Once the egg whites are whisked, you must proceed at once.

Pasta & Rice

Life before pasta seems impossible to imagine. This source of so many quick suppers has been turned into a staple food, inherited from the Chinese via the Italians, whose passion for the stuff knows no bounds. While Italians traditionally have pasta at the beginning of a meal, they too have made it a one-course mid-week meal to be followed by salad, which is the way most of us eat it.

Fresh pasta has been promoted in this country as being somehow superior to the dried variety, a fallacy that has been allowed to continue for too long. Fresh pasta is not necessarily better, it is different. Even in Italy fresh pasta is not eaten that often. Its main drawback in my experience is its delicacy – some fresh pastas cook in seconds and it's a devil of a job to drain, dress and serve it before it becomes overcooked. With a good quality dried pasta, the inherent robustness of the dough can be a distinct advantage and it needs only Parmesan and butter, garlic and oil, or some Ricotta to make a satisfying and speedy meal.

So which pasta to buy? A good Italian deli is the best hunting ground, and after that experiment and see which you prefer. Apart from the shapes, there are two basic types, one made with eggs and the other which is simply durum wheat and water. In Italy pasta manufacture is strictly controlled by law and must conform to set guidelines on ingredients and proportions, but the taste and texture varies with different manufacturers. Don't skimp on the pasta, though. A few pence can mean the difference between something that tastes of nothing, and something that has a rich wheat flavour with good bite.

By all means add oil to the boiling water but in my experience all you need is a large saucepan; sticky pasta has more to do with cosy saucepans and too little water. Parmesan must come off a block of solid cheese – ready grated is not worth buying; it tastes of dust. When you drain the pasta hold back some of the water to add along with the sauce and remember the pasta will go on cooking for a little while after you drain it. When cooking fresh pasta I always add a cup of cold water to slow the cooking down before I drain it, otherwise it is so easy to overcook it.

Rice is more than a food to huge numbers of people, it's a way of life, an essential ingredient in so many diets. It is an amazingly adaptable plant that will grow half-submerged in a rice paddy in the Mekong delta, or 9,000 feet up in the Himalayas. It must have water, but seems able to adapt to extremes of temperature and sunshine, timing its flowering so that it gets enough daylight to allow the grains to ripen. Unlike its colleagues, the other cereal crops, irrigated rice can go on being grown in the same field year after year without exhausting the nutrients in the soil. Some sort of fertiliser or manure is usually applied, but it is thought that some rice fields have been growing this extraordinary crop for thousands of years.

It seems a shame, then, that some of the rice we buy appears to taste of little: an over washed and processed starch accompaniment lurking beneath spoonfuls of curry. It is not for nothing that so many Eastern cultures hold rice in such high esteem. Not only is it a major source of nutrition for many, but the fragrance and richness of plain basmati, Thai, Valencia or any of the Italian risotto rices is an integral part of the recipes in which they are used.

Find a good supplier and give the rice a good smell – it should have a sweet and tempting aroma, the sort that makes you want to have a bowl straight away.

CONCHIGLIE WITH CHORIZO, RED ONION AND TOMATOES

Thick, spicy and earthy, the chorizo sausage is one of Spain's most widely known ingredients, and this dish calls for its marriage to Italy's beloved pasta – one of the better pan-European ideas, in my opinion. Spain and certainly southern Italy share a passion for strong, robust flavours and I detect in a few Italian friends a grudging acceptance that Spain's culinary triumphs are more than a match. Paella versus risotto, Serrano versus Parma, Valencia rice versus Arborio? I'm more than happy to eat on both sides.

SERVES 4

8 chorizo
olive oil
3 red onions, peeled and cut into
  segments (like an orange)
2 garlic cloves, peeled and finely
  chopped
225 g (½ lb) cherry tomatoes

275 ml (½ pint) red wine
2 dessertspoons passata (bottled sieved
  tomatoes)
salt and pepper
450 g (1 lb) conchiglie (pasta shells)
2 tablespoons finely chopped parsley

METHOD: Roughly chop the chorizo and set aside. Heat 4 tablespoons of olive oil in a pan and gently colour the onions for 5 minutes. Add the garlic and chorizo and continue cooking for 5 more minutes, making sure everything is well coated with oil. Add the cherry tomatoes, red wine and passata and a seasoning of salt and pepper. Bring to the boil, lower the heat and simmer, uncovered, for 20 minutes.

Cook the conchiglie in plenty of well-salted water until just done, drain and toss with the sauce, adding the parsley at the same time. Check seasoning and serve.

FETTUCINE WITH CLAMS AND MUSSELS

The mussel, with its plump, succulent flesh, is one of the tastiest of the bivalves – a term which covers all seafood nestling between two hinged shells which can clam shut. In this recipe they are partnered with another favourite: the aptly named clam. If you can get them, Spanish *coquinas* are delicate, sweet and surprisingly meaty. In Sevilla they sit on tapas bars spitting with fury before being turned into a tasty little snack to go with a chilled glass of manzanilla – delicious.

SERVES 4

900 g (2 lb) clams	*1 glass white wine*
900 g (2 lb) mussels	*450 g (1 lb) fettucine*
3 tablespoons finely chopped shallots	*2 tablespoons finely chopped parsley*
1 garlic clove, peeled and finely chopped	*salt and pepper*
olive oil	*1 lemon*

METHOD: Wash the clams and mussels in several changes of cold water, scrubbing the shells to remove any excess grit and barnacles. Sauté the shallots and garlic in 2 tablespoons of olive oil for 5 minutes without colouring. Add the white wine and when it is bubbling, the clams and mussels, strained. Cover and simmer for 3 – 5 minutes, shaking the pan until the bivalves open. Remove from the heat.

Now for the boring part: remove one half of each shell and discard. I tend to get rid of even more shells, leaving at least half the clams and mussels without any shells at all, but it really depends on how much finger licking you wish to do when you are eating. Strain the liquor in the saucepan through a muslin-lined sieve and reserve.

Cook the fettucine in plenty of salted water, drain, dress with a little olive oil and the reserved liquor. Add the clams and mussels, a generous sprinkling of parsley, a little olive oil, salt and lots of pepper and toss thoroughly. Serve with a wedge of lemon.

FETTUCINE WITH KIDNEY SAUCE

I include this recipe as part of my crusade to try and persuade all those who profess not to like lamb kidneys of their rich, robust and delicious qualities. Steak and kidney pie may be a national institution out of step with today's lighter approach to eating, but its presence on restaurant menus, along with calf's liver and sweetbread, convinces me there is a silent majority out there who secretly crave offal. In this recipe the kidney is cut up quite small which may encourage those put off by the shape.

SERVES 4

10 lamb's kidneys
2 tablespoons finely chopped shallots
olive oil
1 garlic clove, finely chopped
1 tablespoon chopped parsley

110 g (4 oz) mushrooms, roughly
*   chopped*
110 ml (4 fl oz) white wine
salt and pepper
450 g (1 lb) dried fettucine

METHOD: Trim the kidneys, removing the fat, gristle and thin membrane. Chop roughly and set aside. Sauté the shallots in 4 tablespoons of olive oil for 5 minutes without colouring. Add the garlic and parsley and cook for a further 5 minutes. Add the mushrooms and toss in the oil, continuing to cook until they start to yield their juices, about 2 minutes. Add the kidneys, sauté for 2 minutes colouring evenly and pour in the white wine. Cook for 2 minutes, remove from the heat, season with salt and pepper and reserve.

Cook the pasta in plenty of boiling salted water, drain and serve with the kidney sauce, which needs to be gently reheated. You may wish to add Parmesan, but I find it a little too strong with the kidneys.

FUSILLI WITH ROASTED PEPPERS
AND SHALLOTS

We think of peppers as being so commonplace and yet even 20 years ago most of us would not have known what to do with these bulbs of red and yellow sweetness. Even Spain and Italy – for us so closely associated with peppers – did not see them until that enterprising Columbus sailed back from America. Now you can find them in most corner stores, thanks to their long shelf life. The addition of a little heat from the grill will have them oozing sweetness in no time.

SERVES 4

2 red peppers
2 yellow peppers
225 g (½ lb) shallots, peeled
olive oil
salt and pepper

1 tablespoon capers, drained and
  gently rinsed
bunch of basil, roughly chopped
450 g (1 lb) fusilli
Parmesan to serve

METHOD: Preheat the grill and cut the peppers into quarters, removing the seeds. Cut the shallots in half. Place shallots – and the peppers, skin side up – under the grill and cook until their surfaces are slightly charred. Remove to a bowl, cover with cling film and set aside. When the peppers are cool enough to handle, remove the skin, cut into strips and return to the bowl with the shallots. Add 5 tablespoons of olive oil, a seasoning of salt and pepper, the capers and basil and toss so they are all well combined.

Cook the pasta until al dente, drain and toss with a little oil. Serve, with the shallots and peppers on top and the Parmesan handed round separately.

LASAGNE OF MUSHROOMS, FONTINA AND HAM

A few years ago the only mushrooms widely available were the tight, hard button variety: a useful addition to a mixed grill, but with very little flavour. Now you can choose between a whole host of cultivated mushrooms – field, brown cap, shitake – or wild varieties like cep, morel and girolle. Even the latter are beginning to appear on supermarket shelves.

SERVES 4

*450 g (1 lb) assorted mushrooms,
   thinly sliced*
olive oil
2 tablespoons finely chopped shallots
2 garlic cloves, finely chopped
50 g (2 oz) cooked ham
1 heaped tablespoon thyme

225 ml (8 fl oz) single cream
*175 g (6 oz) Fontina cheese, roughly
   chopped*
175 ml (6 fl oz) white wine
225 g (8 oz) lasagne sheets
salt and pepper
Parmesan

METHOD: Preheat the oven to gas mark 6/400°F/200°C.

Sauté the mushrooms in 4 tablespoons of olive oil until they start to yield up their juices, about 5 minutes. Stir in the shallots and garlic and continue cooking for a further 5 minutes. Mix the ham and thyme in with the mushrooms and set aside.

In a small saucepan gently heat the cream, Fontina and wine together until the cheese melts. Set aside. Lightly oil a shallow ovenproof dish and alternately layer the pasta, mushrooms and cream sauce, seasoning as you go. Top with a generous sprinkling of Parmesan, cover with tin foil and bake for one hour, removing the foil for the last 10 minutes.

You can reduce the cooking time by pre-cooking the lasagne in boiling salted water before baking.

PAPPARDELLE WITH CHICKEN LIVERS, PINE NUTS AND GREMOLADA

Pappardelle is traditionally served with hare stew, a somewhat time-consuming dish as all the meat has to be boned before you can finish the sauce. The gamy taste is perfect with these wide strips of pasta, however, and chicken livers are a good alternative. Gremolada, a heady mixture of lemon zest, parsley and garlic, is traditionally sprinkled over osso buco just before serving. Used here, it adds a freshness to the taste and brightness of colour to the final dish. If pappardelle is difficult to get hold of, use tagliatelle.

SERVES 4

1 teaspoon finely grated lemon zest
½ teaspoon finely chopped garlic
2 dessertspoons finely chopped parsley
2 tablespoons finely chopped shallots
olive oil
450 g (1 lb) chicken livers, trimmed

2 dessertspoons pine nuts
450 g (1 lb) pappardelle
1 tablespoon brandy
1 glass white wine
salt and pepper
2 tablespoons grated Parmesan

METHOD: Combine the lemon zest, garlic and parsley and set aside in a bowl. Sauté the shallots in olive oil for 5 minutes without colouring. Turn the heat up, add the chicken livers and sauté, continuously stirring, for 5 minutes. Remove from the heat and reserve. Fry the pine nuts in a dry frying pan until lightly coloured and set aside.

Cook the pasta until just al dente, drain and toss with a little olive oil. Return the chicken livers to the heat and when hot, add the brandy, let it sizzle for a few seconds and then stir in the white wine. Bring back to the boil, check seasoning and toss gently with the pasta. Sprinkle over the pine nuts, gremolada and Parmesan.

PAPPARDELLE WITH
WILD MUSHROOMS

Head for the New Forest any weekend in the autumn and you'll find the area alive to the sound of Italian voices. Entire families, spread out in a line, are creeping through the trees, eyes firmly fixed on the ground. Mushrooms are an Italian passion, as they are in many European countries. Not the cultivated ones, but the cep, chanterelle, black trumpet, saffron milk cap and morels that offer exceptional eating. The hunting is great fun and not nearly as dangerous as some people like to make out, although it is better to go the first few times with someone who knows what they are doing. There are a few poisonous mushrooms but they are fairly easy to identify. Use tagliatelle if you are unable to find pappardelle.

SERVES 4

225 g (½ lb) wild mushrooms, finely chopped
olive oil
2 tablespoons finely chopped shallots
2 garlic cloves, peeled and finely chopped
5 tablespoons white wine

50 g (2 oz) chilled butter, cut into cubes
1 dessertspoon thyme
1 tablespoon finely chopped parsley
1 tablespoon double cream
450 g (1 lb) pappardelle
Parmesan to serve

METHOD: Sauté the mushrooms in 4 tablespoons of olive oil for 2 minutes. Add the shallots and garlic and continue frying for about 3 minutes. Add the white wine and continue to cook for a further 2 minutes, or until the wine is almost reduced. Add the butter, thyme and parsley, heat through and stir in the cream.

Cook the pasta in plenty of salted water and serve with the sauce and a little Parmesan.

If you are not keen on hunting wild mushrooms, buy them dried, reconstitute in warm water and mix with cultivated ones. Dried wild mushrooms have a strong flavour, so use about a handful with 225 g (½ lb) cultivated mushrooms.

PASTA PARCELS
WITH POUSSIN AND
LEMON AND LIME BUTTER

Opening these dainty parcels can be a sensual experience. Out comes this cloud of steam heady with the fragrance of lemon and lime followed by the delicious richness of the melting butter. If you are using fresh pasta there is no need to boil it first, but the dried kind need to be loosened up a bit. If it is more convenient you can prepare the parcels in advance and then cook them when everybody is ready – they keep well in the fridge for a few hours.

SERVES 4

4 generous handfuls of tagliatelle	*1 lemon*
2 poussin	*2 limes*
salt and pepper	*bunch of parsley, finely chopped*
175 g (6 oz) butter	

METHOD: Preheat the oven to gas mark 5/375°F/190°C.

If you are using dried pasta, cook briefly in boiling salted water for 2 minutes, drain and refresh under cold water. Divide the pasta into 4 portions and place on 4 squares of double-thickness greaseproof paper.

Split the poussin down the middle, remove the backbone and place on top of the pasta. Season with salt and pepper. Melt the butter in a saucepan and add the grated zest and juice of the lemon and limes, the parsley and a generous seasoning of salt and pepper. Spoon over the poussin and securely fasten each parcel by tightly folding the greaseproof paper several times, sealing the ends with a firm twist. Bake in the oven for 30 minutes, or until the poussin is cooked. Let each person unwrap their own parcel and enjoy the clouds of steam.

PENNE WITH
FRESH SARDINE SAUCE

Driving back from France some years ago we pitched up in Arras for the last few hours of the Saturday morning market, a busy affair that stretches through all of the town's main squares. The fish shop opposite the town hall stays open all day throughout August, catering for *les Anglais* as they hurtle towards the Channel at the end of their holiday. We couldn't resist the sardines, and had them pack half a kilo into bags accompanied by ice. Half a kilo is a lot of sardines and I grilled, roasted and fried my way through them, culminating in a grand finale with this sauce. Nostalgia for a wonderful holiday may have had something to do with it, but I don't think I have ever had such good sardines.

SERVES 4

450 g (1 lb) fresh sardines
2 tablespoons finely chopped shallots
1 garlic clove, peeled and finely chopped
olive oil
2 tablespoons finely chopped parsley

1 dessertspoon thyme
1 dessertspoon roughly chopped capers
salt and pepper
450 g (1 lb) penne
1 lemon

METHOD: Fillet the sardines, which is a very quick operation, by sliding a knife down behind the fish's head and along the backbone. Repeat on the other side and rinse the fillets gently, pat dry and roughly chop. Sauté the shallots and garlic in 2 tablespoons of olive oil for 5 minutes without colouring. Add the sardines, along with the parsley, thyme, capers and a seasoning of salt and pepper. Cook for 5 minutes over a gentle heat and set aside.

Cook the pasta in plenty of boiling salted water, drain and reserve, keeping a little of the water. Toss the pasta in olive oil, tip in the sardine sauce and mix well, so the pasta is coated with the sardine sauce. Serve with a wedge of lemon.

PENNE WITH SALMON, CHILLI AND CAPERS

The days of dumping vats of fish meal into loch-based cages crammed full of salmon are now, thankfully, more or less over. Some of the cages have been towed out to sea, and while the food is still delivered by man, the current-influenced water means the fish have to swim for their supper, building up their muscles which more or less puts paid to that flabby texture evident in some farmed salmon. My preference is still very much for wild fish, but it's expensive and not always available.

Provided you have everything ready, there should be plenty of time to cook the salmon while the pasta is boiling away.

SERVES 4

450 g (1 lb) penne
salt and pepper
450 g (1 lb) salmon, skin removed
*   and cut into 2.5 cm (1 inch)*
*   chunks*
olive oil

4 chillies, deseeded and finely chopped
2 tablespoons capers
75 ml (3 fl oz) white wine
2 tablespoons flat parsley leaves
2 lemons

METHOD: Cook the pasta in plenty of boiling salted water. Meanwhile lightly sauté the salmon in 2 tablespoons of olive oil for 2 minutes, tossing so it is well coloured. Add the chillies and capers, coat in the oil and add the white wine and a seasoning of salt and pepper. Allow to simmer over a moderate heat for 3 minutes, or until the fish is cooked.

Drain the pasta, toss with the salmon and parsley and serve with half a lemon on each plate.

PENNE WITH WINTER PESTO
AND LEMON

The popularity of parsley is curious, given its association with the devil and death. It is said to visit hell seven times before it starts to grow, an explanation for the time it takes to germinate. The Greeks wouldn't have it on the table, so closely was it allied to oblivion. It is a pity we tend to limit its use to decorating food so often: it's full of iron and vitamins and makes a wonderful winter pesto when basil is in short or ropey supply. It is important that the garlic is mashed well – if there are lumps of garlic you will live to regret it.

SERVES 4

*2 generous handfuls of flat-leaf
    parsley, picked over and stalks
    removed*
1 tablespoon shelled walnuts
1 garlic clove, peeled

salt and pepper
2 dessertspoons grated Parmesan
olive oil
2 lemons
450 g (1 lb) penne

METHOD: Blanch the parsley in boiling water for 30 seconds, drain and refresh under cold water, pat dry and put in a pestle and mortar. Add the shelled walnuts, garlic, salt and pepper and mash to a pulp. Add the grated Parmesan and, stirring continuously, dribble in enough olive oil to form a thick, generous paste.

Grate the zest of the lemons, add to their juice and combine with the pesto. Cook the penne in plenty of boiling salted water until al dente, drain and toss with the pesto. Serve with a little more Parmesan.

PIZZOCCHERI

Pizzoccheri, a pasta made partially with buckwheat flour, originates from the Valtellina region of northern Italy. The Venetians, so the story goes, employed the men of Valtellina to build ships for them because of their skill as carpenters. In the sixteenth century a plague wiped out many of the women of Valtellina and to make sure their ships were completed the Venetians gave them their Turkish women slaves. These women are supposed to have arrived carrying sacks of buckwheat flour to which they were rather partial, and slowly a new pasta was created. It contributes a warm, hearty flavour to this dish. You can shorten the cooking time to about 40 minutes if you cook the pizzoccheri in boiling water for 2 minutes beforehand.

SERVES 4

8 unpeeled small potatoes, cut into
    rough chunks
1 small head of Savoy cabbage, cored
    and thinly sliced
2 garlic cloves, finely chopped
50 g (2 oz) butter
olive oil

sprig of fresh sage
4 leeks, trimmed and finely chopped
50 g (2 oz) flour
570 ml (1 pint) milk
salt and pepper
175 g (6 oz) pizzoccheri
175 g (6 oz) strong Cheddar cheese

METHOD: Preheat the oven to gas mark 6/400°F/200°C.

Blanch the potatoes and cabbage together in boiling water for 5 minutes, drain and refresh under cold water. Sauté the garlic in butter with 5 tablespoons of olive oil until just going brown. Strain and discard the garlic. Reheat the oil and briefly fry the sage, drain on kitchen paper and set aside. Add the leeks and soften for 10 minutes, add the flour and cook for 2 minutes without browning. Add the milk and cook for a further 5 minutes, seasoning with salt and pepper.

In a shallow ovenproof dish combine the potatoes, cabbage and pizzoccheri. Season with salt and pepper and add the sage. Add the sauce and arrange the cheese in thin slices on top.

Bake at the top of the oven for 1 hour, or until brown and bubbling. Test the pasta to make sure it is cooked and serve.

RIGATONI WITH RAW TOMATO, RICOTTA AND TARRAGON SAUCE

We all have favourite pasta sauces and this is one that appears in my house all through the summer. Fresh sweet tomatoes must be used and the herb should be in prime condition with an intense fragrance. The ricotta melts on the pasta to a soft creaminess which remains light: perfect for a hot day. Basil works equally well in place of the tarragon.

SERVES 4

225 g (8 oz) Ricotta
10 tomatoes, roughly chopped with the
  core removed (about 225 g / ½ lb
  in weight)
salt and pepper

2 tablespoons grated Parmesan
1 dessertspoon tarragon
olive oil
450 g (1 lb) rigatoni

METHOD: Push the ricotta through a sieve into a bowl and whisk with a wooden spoon. Stir in the tomatoes, a seasoning of salt and pepper, the Parmesan and tarragon and 5 tablespoons of olive oil.

Cook the pasta in plenty of salted water until al dente, drain and toss with the sauce. Serve with extra Parmesan.

RIGATONI WITH ROASTED GARLIC, AUBERGINE AND CAPERS

When you roast garlic its raw astringency takes flight, leaving behind it a clove of melting sweetness, creamy as cheese, sweet as honey. One of my favourite recipes for lamb starts with the words, 'take 50 cloves of garlic'. If you are nervous, blanch the cloves in boiling water for 2 minutes before roasting them. I have seen American restaurant menus where the name of the dish proudly includes the words 'twice-blanched garlic' – reassuring for high-powered lunchtime diners keen to make deals in the afternoon.

SERVES 4

1 head of garlic, split into cloves but unpeeled
2 aubergines, washed and pricked with a fork
1 tablespoon capers, drained and rinsed

salt and pepper
juice of 1 lemon
olive oil
450 g (1 lb) rigatoni
generous handful of rocket
Parmesan for serving

METHOD: Preheat the oven as high as it will go.

Blanch the garlic in boiling water for 2 minutes, drain and refresh under cold water. Arrange the aubergines and garlic in a roasting tin and roast for 40 minutes. Allow to cool slightly and roughly chop the aubergines. Squeeze out the inside of the garlic cloves and add to the aubergine.

Stir in the capers, season with salt and pepper and add lemon juice and olive oil to taste. Cook the pasta in plenty of salted water, drain and toss well with the aubergine mixture. Add the rocket and stir so it wilts slightly. Serve with grated Parmesan.

SPAGHETTI WITH CRAB SAUCE

Crabs are delicious, relatively cheap and remarkably easy to deal with once you get them home. Place the cooked crab on its back, put your fingers round the edge and with your thumbs push the body forward and up. Break off the mouth by pressing downwards, and with this remove the stomach which will come with it. Make sure the gills round the edge are removed and then you are free to eat the rest. If in doubt ask your fishmonger to do the above for you – it's worth watching while he does it. Sprinkle the meat onto some well-dressed salad leaves for a simple and instant supper, or mix with ginger and coriander for a delicious tart.

This pasta dish is a favourite summer recipe, light but also substantial enough when served with a salad and some good bread. If you are in a hurry, buy two dressed crabs, which can be stripped of their meat in seconds. In both cases, the shells make a wonderful stock.

SERVES 4

1 tablespoon finely chopped shallots
olive oil
1 garlic clove, peeled and finely chopped
8 tomatoes
5 tablespoons dry white wine
1 tablespoon finely chopped parsley

110 ml (4 fl oz) fish stock
1 small cooked crab yielding about
* 225 g (½ lb) crab meat*
450 g (1 lb) spaghetti
salt and pepper

METHOD: Sauté the shallots in 2 tablespoons of olive oil for 5 minutes, add the garlic and cook for 2 more minutes. Drop the tomatoes into boiling water for 30 seconds, refresh under cold water and remove the skins and pips. Roughly chop and add to the shallots. Sauté for 5 minutes, add the wine, parsley and fish stock and cook for 5 more minutes.

Cook the pasta in plenty of boiling salted water. Add the crab meat to the tomato sauce, heat through, check seasoning and toss with the cooked and drained pasta.

TAGLIATELLE CON FRATTAGLIE

Frattaglie, or hearts, have a curious and little known property – they all seem to taste the same. I have made this sauce from lamb, pig, boar and beef, and its flavour has been almost identical in each case. I can understand people's reluctance with hearts, but they have a wonderful sweet flavour and it's easy to forget you are eating offal at all. If you need any further reason, they are remarkably cheap, another of those nutritious and delicious cuts of meat that modern taste seems determined to ignore. My thanks to Mauro Bregoli, a superb chef and the owner of The Old Manor House, Romsey, in Hampshire, whose enthusiasm for meat was responsible for persuading me to try hearts in the first place.

SERVES 4

1 onion, peeled and finely chopped
olive oil
1 garlic clove, peeled and finely chopped
50 g (2 oz) unsmoked pancetta or
  streaky bacon, finely chopped
2 carrots, peeled and very finely diced
2 sticks celery, trimmed and finely
  chopped
4 lamb's hearts, coarsely minced

570 ml (1 pint) chicken stock
275 ml (½ pint) red wine
1 × 400 g (14 oz) tin chopped
  tomatoes, drained of their juice
1 tablespoon finely chopped parsley
bunch of thyme
1 bay leaf
450 g (1 lb) tagliatelle
Parmesan

METHOD: Sauté the onion in 4 tablespoons of olive oil for 10 minutes. Add the garlic and pancetta and continue cooking for 5 minutes. Add the carrot and celery and cook for a further 5 minutes. Add the minced heart and sauté for 5 minutes, making sure the meat is well coated in the oil.

Pour in the stock, red wine, tomatoes, parsley, thyme and bay leaf and bring to the boil. Lower the heat and simmer, uncovered, for 1 hour. If the sauce looks like drying out, add a little more water. Remove the bay leaf after the first 20 minutes.

Cook the pasta, toss with the sauce and serve with lots of grated Parmesan.

LIGHTLY SPICED
CHICKEN NOODLE SOUP

A bowl of noodles is just the thing if you want something nourishing to eat and don't want to feel too full afterwards. Buying the spices used to be what put me off but they are now widely available in most of the big supermarkets, often in handy plastic packets. I used to think these were wildly expensive, but my cost-saving visits to ethnic supermarkets usually resulted in a fridge full of dying lemon grass and kaffir lime leaves because I always bought more than I could use.

SERVES 6

1 chicken
2 carrots, peeled and thinly sliced
2 sticks of celery, peeled and thinly
*   sliced*
4 blades of lemon grass
4 kaffir lime leaves
5 cm (2 inch) piece of ginger
1 red chilli
8 black peppercorns

bunch of fresh coriander
salt and pepper
1 tablespoon soy sauce
1 tablespoon fish sauce
1 dessertspoon wakame seaweed
450 g (1 lb) noodles
juice of 1 lemon
bunch of spring onions, finely sliced

METHOD: Put the chicken, breast down, in a saucepan along with the carrots, celery, lemon grass, kaffir lime leaves, half the ginger (sliced), chilli, peppercorns, stems from the coriander and a seasoning of salt and pepper. Cover with water, add the soy sauce and fish sauce and bring to the boil. Lower the heat and simmer for 50 minutes, or until the chicken is cooked. Strain the stock and return to the saucepan. Remove the meat from the chicken.

Bring the stock back to the boil, stir in the seaweed and the noodles and simmer until just done. Return the chicken, season with salt and pepper and add the lemon juice and a generous handful of coriander leaves. Stir in the remaining ginger, grated, along with the spring onions, and serve.

BASMATI RICE WITH SPICED MOONG DAHL, CORIANDER AND CUCUMBER RAITA

I spent some time in India and at every meal I would eat dahl; it became as automatic as having a glass of water. I never tired of its earthy, spicy flavour and there was an added advantage in that the cheaper the restaurant or roadside stall, the better the dahl. I was travelling on a tiny budget and having access to this wonderful food was a godsend. It was always delicious, comforting and nutritious and I still long for it on boiling hot days and cold winter evenings alike. Moong dahl is often sold as mung beans in health food shops. They are small, green and cylindrical.

SERVES 4

175 g (6 oz) moong dahl
1 teaspoon each of ground coriander and cumin
½ teaspoon turmeric
cayenne pepper
4 tablespoons vegetable oil
1 onion, peeled and finely chopped
juice of 2 limes

1 cucumber
1 tablespoon finely chopped spring onion
4 tablespoons yoghurt
bunch of coriander, finely chopped
salt and pepper
450 g (1 lb) basmati rice

METHOD: Soak the moong dahl overnight in the fridge in plenty of water. Combine the coriander, cumin, turmeric and a generous pinch of cayenne pepper with 2 tablespoons of water to make a paste.

Heat the oil in a saucepan and when hot add the onion, sauté for 5 minutes and then add the spice mixture. Cook over a moderate heat for 2 minutes, so the spices release their aromas. Take care they do not burn, or they will go bitter. Add the moong dahl, drained of the water. Pour over 350 ml (12 fl oz) of fresh water, bring to the boil, cover and simmer for 20 minutes, or until the moong dahl is tender. Mash a few tablespoons of the dahl with a fork, then return to the pot and squeeze over the lime juice.

To make the raita, peel, deseed and finely chop the cucumber. Mix with the spring onion, yoghurt and coriander, season with salt and pepper to taste. Cook the rice in plenty of boiling salted water and serve with the dahl and a spoonful of the raita.

BASMATI-STUFFED CHICKEN

Basmati is my favourite rice, its delicately sweet aroma bringing back memories of India like nothing else. The crowded markets, the noise and bustle of Indian life, the serenity of the people, the landscape, but most of all the smell that is India – spices, heat, dust, dung fires and, in the south particularly, always rice. I once spent a year there and, contrary to expectation, managed to put on weight, developing what the Indians call a rice belly. It was worth every inch.

SERVES 4

4 tablespoons cooked basmati rice
4 star anise
3 blades of lemon grass, cut into 7.5 cm (3 inch) lengths
4 kaffir lime leaves

2 cm (1 inch) piece of galangal or ginger, sliced
salt and pepper
1 chicken
50 g (2 oz) butter

METHOD: Preheat the oven to gas mark 6/400°F/200°C.

Combine the rice, star anise, lemon grass, lime leaves and galangal, and season with salt and pepper. Stuff the chicken with this mixture. Rub the butter along the outside of the bird and season with salt and pepper. Roast on its side for 20 minutes, turn on its other side for 20 minutes and finally turn breast-side up for the remaining 20 minutes. Allow to rest for 10 minutes and serve with a spoonful of the lightly aromatic stuffing and the buttery juices from the pan.

BROAD BEAN BROTH WITH
RICE AND PARMESAN

I often cook this dish at the start of the broad bean season, when the evenings are still cool and yet good weather is beckoning just around the corner. I must confess to eating rather too many of the beans raw, before they ever have a chance to reach the pot. On one memorable occasion, a group of us busy depodding ate so many of them, along with a large hunk of Parmesan, there was no point in cooking the dish at all. It was only later that I discovered the Italians consider this a proper course of its own – trouble was, I hadn't much to follow.

SERVES 4

1 onion, peeled and finely chopped
olive oil
1 garlic clove, peeled and finely chopped
50 g (2 oz) pancetta or streaky bacon,
*   finely chopped*
225 ml (8 fl oz) basmati rice
1.25 litres (2 pints) chicken or
*   vegetable stock*

450 g (1 lb) shelled and peeled broad
*   beans*
bunch of thyme
salt and pepper
50 g (2 oz) Parmesan, shaved with a
*   vegetable peeler*

METHOD: Soften the onion in 2 tablespoons of olive oil for 10 minutes, stir in the garlic and pancetta and continue cooking for 2 minutes. Add the rice, coat well in the oil and pour over the stock. Bring to the boil and simmer for five minutes.

Add the beans and thyme, salt and pepper and continue cooking for 5 minutes, or until the rice and beans are tender. Serve in shallow soup plates with a sprinkling of Parmesan and a dribble of olive oil.

GAME RICE

Most of the supermarkets now sell assortment packs of game, containing perhaps three different meats which vary through the year depending on the season. Examples might be venison, rabbit and pigeon; or hare, venison and pheasant; and they are usually made up to a convenient round weight. The different flavours and textures are ideal for this dish and if you are not a game lover, a combination of rabbit, chicken and guinea fowl works equally well, as indeed does a selection of fish. You do need a shallow pan, as the rice must not be too deep, or the dish doesn't work.

SERVES 4

2 onions, peeled and finely chopped
olive oil
2 garlic cloves, peeled and finely
* chopped*
450 g (1 lb) diced game (e.g. venison,
* pigeon and rabbit)*
1 × 400 g (14 oz) tin chopped
* tomatoes, drained of their juice*

1 × 400 g (14 oz) tin haricot beans,
* drained and rinshed*
225 g (½ lb) French beans, trimmed
pinch of saffron
1.25 litres (2 pints) chicken stock
salt and pepper
450 g (1 lb) Valencia rice (or
* short-grain rice)*

METHOD: Sauté the onions in 4 tablespoons of olive oil for 10 minutes, stir in the garlic and continue to cook for a further 2 minutes. Add the meat and lightly colour before adding the tomatoes, beans, saffron, stock and a seasoning of salt and pepper. Bring to the boil, lower the heat and simmer for 20 minutes.

Add the rice and stir into the liquid, turn the heat right down and simmer for 15 minutes, without disturbing, or until most of the liquid has been absorbed by the rice. Check seasoning and serve.

Rice and Lentil Cakes with Coconut and Mustard-seed Chutney

In India these cakes are called vadai. One family I stayed with served them as a Sunday morning treat. At the time I had periodic dreams of bacon and eggs, but as the heat's unrelenting power kept reminding me, the full English breakfast was not really the sort of food required. These cakes are light and sensational with the coconut and mustard-seed chutney. The latter is also good with grilled food in place of some of the more usual sauces.

SERVES 4 AS A FIRST COURSE

110 g (4 oz) grated coconut
4 green chillies, tops removed and chopped
5 shallots, peeled and roughly chopped
5 cm (2 inch) piece of ginger, finely chopped
handful of mint leaves
vegetable oil
1 teaspoon mustard seeds

225 g (8 oz) urad dahl, soaked overnight (available from ethnic supermarkets)
2 tablespoons uncooked rice, soaked overnight
2 onions, peeled and finely chopped
1/2 teaspoon cumin seeds
salt and pepper

METHOD: Put the coconut, two of the chillies, the shallots, half the ginger and mint leaves in a liquidiser and blend to a smooth paste. Heat 1 tablespoon of oil in a frying pan and lightly brown the mustard seeds. Remove from the heat, add the coconut paste from the liquidiser, stir and set aside.

Liquidise the dahl and rice to form a paste. If necessary, add a little water, but beware, too much and the cakes will fall apart when you fry them. Combine with the onion, cumin seeds, remaining ginger and chillies and a generous pinch of salt. Heat 5 cm (2 inches) of oil in a suitable pan, shape the dough into flat golf balls and deep-fry until just golden. Drain on kitchen paper and serve with the chutney.

RICE AND CHICKPEA STEW WITH RED ONIONS, SHERRY VINEGAR AND TOASTED ALMONDS

Sherry vinegar started life as an accident, the result of a sherry butt having gone off. Soon, however, the housewives of Jerez were demanding more and the sherry producers had to spoil butts on purpose to keep up with demand. Sherry is one of my favourite drinks. Bone dry finos, fine manzanillas, rich olorosos – it's an infinite world of superb wine so far removed from aunty's favoured sweet tipple as to be unrecognisable. Buy half a bottle, slip it into the fridge and pour yourself a glass when you arrive home, or allow a full bottle and drink it with a dish like this, which is what the Spanish would do.

SERVES 4

4 red onions, peeled and quartered
olive oil
2 garlic cloves, peeled and finely
  chopped
2 tablespoons sherry vinegar
1.25 litres (2 pints) vegetable or
  chicken stock

1 × 400 g (14 oz) tin chickpeas,
  drained and rinsed
175 ml (6 fl oz) rice
salt and pepper
1 bay leaf
2 tablespoons toasted flaked almonds

METHOD: Gently sauté the red onions in 5 tablespoons of olive oil for 15 minutes, or until they just begin to colour. Add the garlic, continue to cook for 2 minutes and then splash in the vinegar, which will spit a bit. Pour in the stock and the chickpeas and bring to the boil.

Pour in the rice, season with salt and pepper and add the bay leaf. Bring back to boiling point, lower the heat and simmer for 15–20 minutes, or until the rice is just cooked. Remove the bay leaf and serve with the almonds sprinkled on top.

LADIES' RICE

In the days before equality, this dish was known in Spain as ladies' rice, the absence of bones being considered suitable for damsels while the supposedly more macho males were told to roll up their sleeves and get on with the bone-laden version. Being a passionate devotee of finger food I used to feel rather sorry for the ladies, thinking they couldn't have had as much fun and their version would have lacked the sweetness and body the bones contribute. Fernando Cordoba then cooked the dish for me in Andalucia one brilliantly sunny autumn day and I was proved wrong – the dish is sensational, a brilliant marriage of rice and fish. I have adapted his original recipe.

SERVES 4

1.25 litres (2 pints) fish stock
pinch of saffron
4 whole garlic cloves
½ teaspoon paprika
450 g (1 lb) Valencia rice
2 red peppers, cored, deseeded and cut
into thin strips

2 garlic cloves, peeled and finely
chopped
1 tablespoon chopped shallots
olive oil
900 g (2 lb) assorted fish
2 lemons, halved

METHOD: Preheat the oven to gas mark 5/375°F/190°C.

Bring the fish stock to simmering point and add the saffron, whole garlic and paprika. Allow to simmer for 10 minutes. Meanwhile sauté the rice, red peppers, chopped garlic and shallots in 5 tablespoons of olive oil over a gentle heat for 5 minutes in a shallow ovenproof pan. Stir in the fish and pour over the fish stock, removing the garlic cloves as you do, and season with salt and pepper.

Bring to simmering point and transfer to the oven. Bake for 20 minutes, remove and serve with lemon to squeeze over.

THREE-FISH KEDGEREE

Kedgeree is stolen property, a theft committed by the Raj during their sojourn in that vast and wonderful continent and subsequently institutionalised into a bin for all the leftovers, part of the reason for its unjust downfall. In fact, this is a delicate and subtle dish worthy of much more attention. Ingredients for the original Indian version included lentils, rice and spices, a nourishing blend of relatively inexpensive ingredients eaten by Indians in their thousands. A forkful of this quintessentially Victorian dish should contain, according to popular belief, some rice, a little smoked haddock, some onion, some spices, butter, a little chopped parsley and, if you're lucky, some hard-boiled egg. In this version I have included three contrasting types of fish – fresh water, sea and smoked – all of which contribute something slightly different.

SERVES 4

225 g (½ lb) fresh salmon	*cumin and garam masala*
225 g (½ lb) trout or char	*pinch of cayenne pepper*
450 g (1 lb) smoked haddock	*pinch of saffron*
450 g (1 lb) long-grain rice	*salt and pepper*
50 g (2 oz) finely chopped shallots	*1 tablespoon finely chopped parsley*
olive oil	*4 eggs*
1 teaspoon each ground coriander,	

METHOD: Poach the fish in a court bouillon (see below) for 4 minutes, or until almost cooked, drain and flake the fish. Cook the rice until tender, about 15 minutes, drain and refresh under cold water to stop it cooking.

Soften the shallots in 4 tablespoons of olive oil for 5 minutes. Stir in the spices, but not the saffron, and continue cooking, stirring all the time, for a further 5 minutes, taking care nothing catches. If there is any danger, stir in a dessertspoon of water and carry on cooking. Add the rice, saffron and fish, season well with salt and pepper and gently heat through, stirring in the parsley as you do so.

Poach the eggs and serve on top of the rice and fish mixture. An alternative way of serving this is to pack the rice mixture into lightly oiled ramekins, chill and then turn out on to a plate and serve with hollandaise instead of poached eggs.

> **To make a court bouillon:** combine spices like peppercorns with vegetables (e.g. celery, carrots, leeks and onions) and a little vinegar. Add sufficient water and bring to the boil.

WILD MUSHROOM RISOTTO

Risotto is my ultimate comfort food; soothing, encouraging, full of subtle flavours that blend together to produce a homogeneous whole. Cooking may be a craft rather than an art, but when I'm making risotto I feel about as close to an easel as I'm ever likely to get. For all my enthusiasm, it took me quite a few years before I got round to making risotto. The idea of simmering pans of stock and constantly ladling it into the rice all seemed like a lot of bother. Like so much in cooking, however, do it once or twice slowly, and you soon get the hang of it. As for the time taken, with a bit of luck I aim to get risotto on the table in about 40 minutes, which is one reason why it is rarely good in restaurants. This is the master recipe, with ideas for variations following after. If you are making up your own, it's worth restricting the ingredients to two or three, otherwise you tend to get a clash of flavours.

SERVES 4

50 g (2 oz) dried porcini mushrooms
1 onion, peeled and finely chopped
olive oil
1.25 litres (2 pints) chicken or
    vegetable stock

275 g (10 oz) Arborio rice
50 g (2 oz) butter
½ glass vermouth
Parmesan
salt and pepper

METHOD: Put the mushrooms in a bowl of hot water and set aside. Soften the onion in 3 tablespoons of olive oil over a gentle heat for at least 10 minutes, more like 15. The onions need to release their juice and taste sweet. Heat the stock in a separate saucepan until boiling, lower the heat and allow to simmer. Stir the rice into the onions and coat in the oil, continuing to cook over a moderate heat for 2 minutes. Remove the mushrooms from the soaking water and pour this into the simmering stock, taking care to leave the grit behind.

Add 2 ladlefuls of stock to the rice, stirring all the time so none of the rice sticks to the bottom, lower the heat and continue to cook, adding a ladle of stock each time the rice almost dries out. Continue until the rice is cooked, about 15 to 20 minutes. If you run out of stock, add boiling water instead.

About 5 minutes before the end, stir in the mushrooms. When the rice is cooked – remember it goes on cooking while it's sitting in the pan, which is one reason why everyone should already be sitting down – stir in the butter, vermouth and a tablespoon of grated Parmesan. Season and serve with a bowl of grated Parmesan for people to serve themselves.

Ideas for risottos:

In each case stir these ingredients into the risotto as you would the mushrooms in the previous recipe.

Butternut squash: Peel, deseed and cut one butternut squash into 2.5 cm (1 inch) chunks. Place in a roasting tray, dribble over a little olive oil and season with salt and pepper. Roast in a preheated oven, gas mark 7/425°F/220°C, for 30 minutes, or until tender and roughly chop.

Saffron and roast red pepper: Grill the peppers until charred, remove to a bowl and cover with cling film for 10 minutes, peel and deseed. Stir, along with a generous pinch of saffron, into the risotto.

Radicchio and red wine: Sauté 2 heads of radicchio, cored and roughly sliced, in 2 tablespoons of olive oil for 5 minutes. Pour in 225 ml (8 fl oz) of red wine and reduce for 10 minutes over a moderate heat.

Pea and broad bean: Shell both and remove the skin from the broad beans so you have 110 g (4 oz) of each.

Fennel and pastis: Trim 2 fennel bulbs top and bottom and placing the base of the fennel on a board, cut thin slices downwards. Blanch in boiling water for 2 minutes, drain and refresh. Sauté with 50 g (2 oz) of butter in a covered pan over a moderate heat until tender, about 10 minutes. Pour in a glass of pastis, set it alight and wait for the flames to die down.

Jerusalem artichokes: Peel and cook in plenty of boiling water with a squeeze of lemon juice until just tender. Roughly chop and add to the risotto.

RISOTTO CAKES WITH BROCCOLI, SHAVED PARMESAN AND ARTICHOKES

I am hopeless at throwing out food. However small the amount left over, it goes into a bowl, is wrapped in cling film and put in the fridge because I always think it might come in handy. This is often followed several days later by a reverse action: out of the fridge, remove cling film, put in bin and wash up bowl. None of this happens with leftover risotto, however, which fries up into delicious cakes and makes a remarkably quick meal to follow the previous endless stirring and stock-adding which is an essential part of a risotto.

Make sure you buy a good quality jar of artichokes – there are a lot of tasteless varieties around.

SERVES 4

approximately 450 g (1 lb) leftover risotto
450 g (1 lb) broccoli
salt and pepper

1 jar globe artichokes in oil
olive oil
50 g (2 oz) shaved Parmesan
2 lemons

METHOD: Dip your hand in water, then shape the risotto into balls using a spoon and the palm of your hand. Refrigerate. Cook the broccoli in plenty of boiling salted water until almost cooked, then briefly refresh under cold water and set aside. Finely slice the artichokes.

Arrange the broccoli on 4 plates. Fry the risotto cakes in 2 tablespoons of olive oil until lightly browned all over. Place on top of the broccoli, scatter the artichokes and dribble over a little olive oil and the Parmesan. Serve with half a lemon per person and a seasoning of salt and pepper.

Vegetables

I enjoy shopping for vegetables more than any other ingredient – all the colours, textures and shapes make for such variety that I find it difficult not to let rip and buy them all. Salads eaten raw, steamed root vegetables, roasted red peppers, grilled courgettes – there seems no end to the list and just when you think you have exhausted it, a new season begins and different things start to appear.

I still find it odd to imagine that only 20 years ago the wealth of variety available to us now did not exist. Peppers were strange, courgettes unheard of and aubergines attracted intense suspicion. Garlic was to be avoided and artichokes, fennel, okra, rocket, beansprouts and sweetcorn were strange names to be found in books rather than on the shelves of local supermarkets. Seasons were defined and unchanging, quality was often variable and consistency of supply a constant problem.

Since then we have rocketed through tasteless tomatoes, boring potatoes, frozen peas and button mushrooms. Now we have tomatoes grown for flavour, old varieties of potato reappearing, fresh peas and broad beans sold in the pod and even wild mushrooms sold in some of the supermarkets. Year-round asparagus is a fact – if you like that kind of thing – as are French beans (not often from France), aubergines, courgettes and peppers of all colours. We have never had it so good.

I am still driven by the seasons, however, preferring to celebrate summer with the first of the English – and surely the best – asparagus, heaping hollandaise on the early sprouting broccoli when the summer heat has still not quite established itself; and in autumn watching evenings grow shorter to the smell of roasting chestnuts, parsnip soups and sautéing leeks. Cucumber may be available in November, but watch its price tumble and quality soar for the brighter months. Savoy cabbage tastes infinitely better with the threat of the first frost while the abundance of courgettes and tomatoes towards the end of summer is enough reason to eat nothing else.

The following recipes are mostly suitable for vegetarians, although a few do contain meat. All are dishes that I eat regularly, the sort of food that inspires with its colour and does not take too long to prepare. With fresh vegetables the less-is-more approach to cooking them is usually the only way to maintain their vibrancy.

STUFFED AUBERGINE

I am frequently asked about salting aubergines. For what it's worth, I rarely do. I have tried both ways in the same recipe with no discernible difference. Some people still swear by salting, arguing it removes the bitterness, but the modern aubergine seems to have grown out of that nasty phase.

SERVES 4

4 aubergines
450 g (1 lb) small new potatoes,
  washed
2 garlic cloves, peeled
1 onion, peeled and roughly chopped
4 tomatoes

vegetable oil
2 teaspoons ground cumin
bunch fresh coriander, leaves removed
  and stalks finely chopped
175 ml (6 fl oz) yoghurt
salt and pepper

METHOD: Prick the aubergines and potatoes and bake in a preheated oven gas mark 5/375°F/190°C for 30 minutes, or until cooked (the aubergines take about 20 minutes, the potatoes 30 minutes or slightly longer). Put the garlic, onion and 3 tablespoons of water into a liquidiser and blend. Drop the tomatoes into boiling water for 20 seconds, refresh under cold water and peel and deseed.

Remove the flesh from the aubergines, taking care not to puncture the skins, and roughly chop along with the potatoes. I leave the skin on the potatoes, but you may wish to remove it. Heat 3 tablespoons of oil in a frying pan, tip in the onion and garlic mixture along with the ground cumin and fry gently for 5 minutes. Stir in the potatoes and aubergine and cook for 5 minutes. Stir in the tomatoes, coriander stalks and yoghurt and remove from the heat. Season with salt and pepper and stuff the aubergine skins. Return to the oven and cook for a further 15 minutes, or until heated through and golden brown on top. Serve with a sprinkling of coriander leaves.

Grilled leeks with anchovy and chopped-egg salad *(page 17)*

Fettucine with clams and mussels *(page 25)*

Fusilli with roasted peppers and shallots *(page 27)*

Risotto cakes with broccoli, shaved Parmesan and artichokes *(page 51)*

Grilled radicchio with brioche and mushrooms *(page 83)*

Roast
Mediterranean
vegetables with polenta and
black olive dressing *(page 87)*

Roast butternut squash with green bean and black olive salad *(page 93)*

Caviar, crème fraîche and potato blinis *(page 104)*

AUBERGINE, BASIL AND YOGHURT SALAD

Basil, originally from India and traditionally found in every Hindu house-hold, is the herb I most associate with summer. Sweet, powerful and yet so delicate, its perfume is guaranteed to put everyone in a good mood, one of the reasons why it was initially used in this country, not as a culinary herb, but as an ingredient in sweet waters, scent bags and nosegays. 'We in England greatly esteem it because it smelleth sweet, and (as some think) comforteth the brain.' (John Swain in *Speculum Mundi.*)

SERVES 4

2 aubergines	*225 g (½ lb) spinach leaves*
olive oil	*1 garlic clove*
a large handful of basil leaves	*salt and pepper*
175 ml (6 fl oz) yoghurt	*50 g (2 oz) pine nuts*
4 tomatoes, sliced	*1 lemon*

METHOD: Cut the aubergines across into slices about ½ cm (¼ inch) thick and lightly brush with olive oil. Grill until slightly charred and transfer to a bowl. Roughly chop the basil leaves and add these, along with 5 tablespoons of olive oil, the yoghurt, tomatoes and spinach leaves, to the bowl. Peel and mash the garlic with ½ teaspoon each of salt and pepper and add this to the aubergine.

Heat a frying pan without any oil and when hot toast the pine nuts until they just begin to colour. Add these to the bowl, toss everything well, squeeze over the juice of the lemon and serve with lots of bread.

GRILLED AUBERGINE WITH
EGG NOODLES AND BEANSPROUTS

We have grown used to the dark, forbidding oblong-shaped vegetable that we call aubergine but in fact this vegetable comes in numerous forms and colours. In Thailand the aubergine is the size and shape of a pea, in its other forms it can be round, squat and pumpkin-shaped, or long and oval. Colours range from the familiar dark blue-black to a marbling of grey green – proof that this vegetable was once grown not for its delicious flesh, but for decoration.

SERVES 6

4 red peppers
2 aubergines
sesame seed oil
soy sauce
salt and pepper

110 g (4 oz) beansprouts
2.5 cm (1 inch) piece of ginger
450 g (1 lb) Chinese egg noodles
bunch of spring onions

METHOD: Grill the peppers until the skin is charred, remove to bowl and cover with cling film or a damp cloth. Slice the aubergines lengthways into ½ cm (¼ inch) slices and grill on each side until lightly charred. Allow to cool and then cut into short strips as thinly as possible. Toss the aubergine with 5 tablespoons of sesame seed oil, 3 tablespoons of soy sauce and a seasoning of salt and pepper. Add the beansprouts and the ginger, peeled and cut into thin julienne strips. Peel and deseed the peppers, roughly tear and add to the aubergine.

Cook the noodles in plenty of salted water until tender. Meanwhile, finely slice the spring onions including most of the green part. Toss the noodles with the aubergine mixture, top with the spring onions and serve.

BROAD BEAN MOUSSE WITH
CRISPY SAGE AND SPINACH SALAD

Broad beans have been grown throughout Europe for as long as anyone can remember. If you were offered beans on toast in the first century AD, your host would have meant broad beans, for that was all there was available. It was only when Christopher Columbus brought back kidney and haricot beans from the New World that the word bean needed a qualifier. I still remain faithful to the broad bean. Even in its dried form, it is perhaps the most delicious bean of all.

SERVES 4

900 g (2 lb) shelled and peeled broad beans	*2 tablespoons chopped parsley*
salt and pepper	*4 eggs, separated*
50 g (2 oz) butter	*olive oil*
4 tablespoons chopped shallots	*bunch of sage*
1 garlic clove, peeled and finely chopped	*225 g (½ lb) uncooked spinach*
pinch of cayenne pepper	*bunch of spring onions*
	1 tablespoon sesame seeds

METHOD: Preheat the oven to gas mark 5/375°F/190°C.

Cook the beans in boiling salted water until tender, drain, refresh under cold water, pat dry and set aside. Melt the butter in a frying pan and gently sauté the shallots for 5 minutes until soft and slightly caramelised. Add the garlic and continue cooking for 2 minutes. Purée the beans – you may need a little extra water – and add to the shallots, along with the cayenne pepper. Season with salt and pepper, cover, and cook over a gentle heat for 5 minutes.

Put the bean mixture into a bowl, and stir in the parsley and egg yolks. Whisk the egg white until stiff and then gently fold in the bean mixture. Divide the mixture into four size-two ramekins, about 8 cm (3¼ inches) in diameter. Pour boiling water into a roasting tin so it comes halfway up the side of the ramekins and bake for 25 minutes, or until set.

Heat 2–3 tablespoons of olive oil in a frying pan and when hot, tip in the sage leaves – they only take 10–15 seconds to crisp up. Remove and drain on kitchen paper. Toss the spinach with a little of the olive oil when it has cooled slightly. Finely chop the spring onions and add these, along with the sesame seeds, to the spinach. Turn the mousse out on top of the spinach salad and serve with the sage sprinkled on top of the mousse.

BROAD BEAN FALAFELS WITH RED ONION AND CUMIN SALSA

Depending on which country you stop off in around the Mediterranean, falafels are either made with chickpeas or broad beans. My own preference is for the latter, partly for the colour, which is a most mouthwatering green, and partly for the subtle taste which is a bit richer than chickpeas. You need the dried, skinless variety, usually available from better delicatessens. If you can't get broad beans, however, chickpeas are also delicious and can be substituted in this recipe.

SERVES 4

*2 red onions, peeled and cut into fine
  half-moon slices*
salt and pepper
2 teaspoons cumin seeds
bunch each of coriander and parsley
olive oil

*225 g (½ lb) dried and skinned broad
  beans, soaked overnight*
2–3 garlic cloves, finely chopped
1 onion, finely chopped
cayenne pepper

METHOD: Put the red onion in a sieve with 2 dessertspoons of salt. Set aside for 10 minutes, rinse under plenty of cold water and pat dry. Roast the cumin seeds in a hot dry frying pan for 30 seconds, making sure they don't stick and burn. Add to the red onions along with a tablespoon of roughly chopped fresh coriander leaves, a seasoning of pepper and 2 tablespoons of olive oil. Set aside.

Liquidise the beans until they become a smooth paste. You may need to add a little water, but no more than a tablespoon, or the falafels won't form into balls. Stir in a heaped tablespoon each of chopped coriander and parsley, the garlic, onion and a pinch of cayenne pepper. Put the mixture in the fridge for 30 minutes and then form into balls.

Heat 5 tablespoons of oil in a frying pan and sauté the falafels until golden. Drain on kitchen paper and serve warm with the red onion and cumin salsa. You may need to add a little more oil as you make your way through the mixture.

BROCCOLI, BLACK OLIVES AND PARMESAN WITH WARM ANCHOVY DRESSING

The spring and early summer are the times for feasting on sprouting broccoli: for the rest of the year the more closely packed cauliflower-like calabrese is the one to use (although I have to confess a preference for the sprouting kind). Whichever vegetable you buy, you'll discover that this is one of the best boiled vegetable salads we have. Try and get hold of young broccoli. The stems should be sweet and succulent – woodiness is for trees.

SERVES 4

900 g (2 lb) broccoli
salt and pepper
110 g (4 oz) pitted black olives
110 g (4 oz) Parmesan
50 g (2 oz) anchovies (the white variety available in Italian delicatessens –

the brown tinned sort tend to be too salty)
1 garlic clove, peeled and finely minced
olive oil
1 lemon

METHOD: Steam or boil the broccoli until just cooked, drain and refresh under cold water, arrange on a large plate and season with salt and pepper. Sprinkle over the black olives and 50 g (2 oz) of the Parmesan, grated. Cut the remaining Parmesan into shavings using a vegetable peeler.

Mash the anchovies, garlic and a seasoning of salt and pepper together and whisk in 110 ml (4 fl oz) of olive oil and lemon juice to taste. Pour over the broccoli, scatter the Parmesan shavings and serve.

SPROUTING BROCCOLI SALAD WITH QUAIL'S EGGS AND PECORINO

Sprouting broccoli used to be sold in the same way as asparagus, stems bunched and tied attractively to be rushed home and cooked. Try it with hollandaise sauce or home-made mayonnaise: it's a boiled feast and all the more delicious because it doesn't cost the earth and isn't, like asparagus, with us throughout the year. Aged Pecorino is similar to, although not the same as, Parmesan. You can substitute the latter, if Pecorino is hard to find, although it is becoming increasingly popular.

SERVES 4

1 dozen quail's eggs
3 thin slices of garlic
salt and pepper
olive oil
balsamic vinegar

4 handfuls of various salad leaves
110 g (4 oz) mature Pecorino
450 g (1 lb) purple sprouting broccoli,
*   trimmed of any tough stalk ends*

METHOD: Boil the quail's eggs for 2 minutes, drain and refresh under cold water, peel and set aside.

Mash the garlic with a seasoning of salt and pepper until it becomes a pulp. There must be no whole bits of garlic, so sea salt and coarsely ground pepper is best for this. Stir in 5 tablespoons of olive oil and a dessertspoon of balsamic vinegar. Toss the leaves in this dressing. Peel the Pecorino into slivers with a vegetable peeler.

Cook the broccoli in a large pan of boiling salted water for 5 minutes, or until just tender. Drain and refresh briefly under cold water – it should still be warm. Toss the broccoli in with the salad leaves and coat in the dressing. Distribute on 4 plates, scatter over the quail's eggs and Pecorino and serve.

CABBAGE PARCELS WITH RICOTTA, TOASTED ALMONDS, PARSLEY AND SAGE

The king of cabbages is without doubt the Savoy: crisp green leaves with the most divine wrinkles and a strong flavour. Whether briefly cooked so it still retains its crunch, or slowly stewed with spices, this is a vegetable with bags of flavour. This recipe makes good use of the outside leaves; there aren't many instances where you can feast so well on the wrapping.

SERVES 4

8 outside leaves from a Savoy cabbage	*olive oil*
450 g (1 lb) ricotta	*1 garlic clove, peeled and sliced*
75 g (3 oz) grated Parmesan	*1 dessertspoon fresh sage leaves*
110 g (4 oz) toasted almonds	*salt and pepper*
2 tablespoons chopped parsley	

METHOD: Preheat the oven to gas mark 4/350°F/180°C.

Remove the tough central core of each cabbage leaf and blanch the leaves in salted boiling water for 2 minutes. Drain and refresh under cold water. Combine the ricotta, Parmesan, toasted almonds and parsley in a bowl.

Heat 5 tablespoons of olive oil in a pan and when hot, but not smoking, add the garlic. Fry until golden, remove and discard. Add the sage leaves and fry for 20 seconds, remove and drain on kitchen paper. Allow the oil to cool and then whisk into the Ricotta mixture, along with the roughly chopped sage leaves and a seasoning of salt and pepper.

Divide the mixture up among the cabbage leaves, roll up and secure with a cocktail stick. Arrange the cabbage parcels on an ovenproof dish, cover with tin foil and bake for 20 minutes. Serve with the remaining cabbage, shredded and stir-fried, and rice or potatoes.

CARROT AND CORIANDER MOUSSE WITH
WATERCRESS AND ORANGE SALAD

Carrots appear commonplace to us, but in the time of the Stuarts ladies pinned carrot tops to their bosoms in place of feathers and their hats were likewise plummaged with this exotic vegetable, although it was not like the modern variety we know today. For us bright orange is a prerequisite and that only came about when a purple carrot from Afghanistan was crossed with what Jane Grigson describes as a yellow mutant. Commonplace or not, the partnership of carrots with coriander is hard to beat.

SERVES 4

1 onion, finely chopped	*salt and pepper*
olive oil	*2 eggs, separated*
450 g (1 lb) carrots, trimmed, peeled	*bunch of fresh coriander*
and roughly chopped	*4 handfuls of watercress*
50 g (2 oz) butter	*1 orange, peeled and segmented*
2 teaspoons ground coriander	*1 lemon*

METHOD: Preheat the oven to gas mark 4/350°F/180°C.

Sauté the onion in 2 tablespoons of olive oil without colouring for 10 minutes. Add the carrots, butter and ground coriander, cover and continue cooking for 10 minutes – add a few drops of water if it looks like catching. Remove from the heat, season with salt and pepper and set aside.

Whisk the egg whites until stiff and fold into the carrot mixture along with the egg yolks and 2 tablespoons of chopped fresh coriander. Spoon into 4 dariole moulds and place in a baking tin. Pour in boiling water to come halfway up the moulds and bake for 25 minutes or until set. Allow to cool to just above room temperature.

Toss the watercress with the orange segments, 2–3 tablespoons of olive oil, a seasoning of salt and pepper and lemon juice to taste. Arrange on 4 plates, turn the carrot mousses out on top of the leaves and garnish with fresh coriander leaves.

CELERIAC ROSTI WITH FENNEL AND BLACK OLIVE SALAD

Celeriac is not exactly the most handsome vegetable, with its light brown colouring and rotund shape, but underneath the surface lurks the most delicious flavour, a cross between turnip and celery with all the crunch of a radish. Grated into spaghetti-like strands and dressed with a hot mustard mayonnaise it becomes remoulade, a superior coleslaw. This recipe is another way of enjoying this overlooked vegetable, although celeriac dauphinoise is also a favourite.

SERVES 4

1 celeriac (about 450 g/ 1 lb in weight)
1 onion, finely chopped
1 dessertspoon finely chopped thyme
salt and pepper
50 g (2 oz) melted butter
2 eggs, lightly beaten

Pernod or similar
450 g (1 lb) spinach
2 fennel bulbs
110 g (4 oz) pitted black olives
juice of 1 lemon
olive oil

METHOD: Peel and grate the celeriac on the largest holes of your grater and wash in plenty of cold water. Drain, pat dry and mix with the onion, thyme and a seasoning of salt and pepper. Mix with the melted butter and eggs and refrigerate.

Bring 110 ml (4 fl oz) of Pernod to the boil, carefully set alight and burn off the alcohol; set aside. Blanch the spinach in boiling water for 30 seconds, drain and refresh under cold water. Trim the fennel top and bottom and slice as thinly as possible. Blanch in boiling water for 4 minutes, drain and refresh under cold water. Combine the spinach and fennel with the black olives, lemon juice, salt and pepper and 5 tablespoons of olive oil, the Pernod and set aside.

You need a flat-bottomed sturdy cup, a ramekin or, ideally, four circular pastry cutters. Put a generous amount of the celeriac into whatever utensil you are using and tip it into 110 ml (4 fl oz) of hot olive oil. You should end up with four neat circles in an average-sized frying pan. Gently sauté for 5 minutes, turn over and repeat the other side. Serve on top of the spinach and fennel salad.

CHEESE AND HERB PUFFS WITH
TOMATO AND RED ONION SALAD

One of the most exciting developments in British food over the last few years has been the enormous explosion in farmhouse cheeses. Where 10 years ago we were a nation gorging ourselves on the delights of French cheese, there are now entire shops devoted to cheese from within these islands – in many cases better or at least on a par with what the French feast on. Let them multiply, for we cannot ever have enough good cheese.

SERVES 4

1 red onion, peeled and finely chopped
salt and pepper
60 g (2½ oz) butter
150 g (5 oz) plain flour
4 eggs
110 g (4 oz) of any medium strong
  cheese, grated

1 dessertspoon each of parsley,
  tarragon, chives and thyme
8 tomatoes
5 tablespoons olive oil
juice of ½ a lemon
bunch of basil

METHOD: Sprinkle the onion with plenty of salt and put in a sieve over a bowl for 5 minutes. Rinse in plenty of cold water and pat dry.

Preheat the oven to gas mark 5/375°F/190°C. Combine 225 ml (8 fl oz) of water with a pinch of salt and the butter in a saucepan. Place over a medium heat, bring to the boil and as soon as the butter is melted, remove from the heat. Add the flour all at once, stirring with a wooden spoon. Return to the heat, stir vigorously, then beat until the mixture pulls away from the side of the pan in a smooth mass. Remove from the heat and allow to cool for 2 or 3 minutes.

Beat in the eggs, whole, one at a time, continuing to beat each time until the egg is completely incorporated and the paste is smooth before adding the next egg. Add the cheese and herbs at the same time as the last egg and beat well.

At 7.5 cm (3 inch) intervals, drop teaspoons of the paste on to a baking sheet and bake for 25 minutes, or until cooked. Slice the tomatoes, mix with the onion, olive oil, lemon juice and salt and pepper. Divide on to 4 plates, sprinkle with the basil leaves and place the cheese and herb puffs on top.

GOAT'S CHEESE AND WALNUT PITHIVIERS WITH CHERRY TOMATO SAUCE

Pithiviers, originally from the town of the same name in France, are large round puff-pastry tarts filled with almond cream and sporting scalloped edges. They were traditionally served on Twelfth Night, when a fava bean would be inserted, quite why I'm not sure. It can't have been that pleasant to come across a fava bean in the middle of a whole pile of almond cream. These mini savoury versions are equally creamy, with some earthy walnuts to replace the almonds.

SERVES 4

25 g (1 oz) butter	*225 g (8 oz) puff pastry*
1 tablespoon plain flour	*2 eggs, separated*
150 ml (5 fl oz) milk	*50 g (2 oz) shelled walnuts*
salt and pepper	*225 g (½ lb) cherry tomatoes, roughly*
nutmeg	*chopped*
110 g (4 oz) goat's cheese	*110 ml (4 fl oz) olive oil*
cayenne pepper	*2 teaspoons balsamic vinegar*

METHOD: Preheat the oven to gas mark 6/400°F/200°C.

Heat the butter, flour and milk gently until thickened. Carry on cooking without colouring for 5 minutes. Season with salt and pepper and a grating of nutmeg, and gently melt the goat's cheese into the sauce, which must not now boil. Season with a pinch of cayenne pepper and set aside.

Roll out half the pastry and cut out eight 6 cm (2¼ inch) circles, then use the remainder of the pastry to make eight 7 cm (2¾ inch) circles. Mix the egg yolks and walnuts in with the cheese mixture. Whisk the egg whites until stiff and fold into the cheese and walnut mixture. Spoon on to the smaller size pastry discs, leaving a small border. Brush the edges with a little milk and cover with the larger pastry discs. Press down the edges with a fork, prick the tops 2 or 3 times and bake on a lightly greased baking tray for 20 minutes, or until golden brown.

Combine the cherry tomatoes, olive oil and balsamic vinegar, season with salt and pepper and serve with the pithiviers on top.

GOAT'S CHEESE SOUFFLÉ WITH SPINACH AND SUN-DRIED TOMATO DRESSING

Search out a strong goat's cheese for this recipe, something crumbly, with age and character. The egg dilutes the flavour, so you need something with bite.

SERVES 4

50 g (2 oz) butter, plus a little extra to butter the dish
25 g (1 oz) plain flour
275 ml (½ pint) milk
4 eggs, separated
110 g (4 oz) goat's cheese, crumbled
salt and pepper

cayenne pepper
2 handfuls breadcrumbs
4 sun-dried tomatoes
olive oil
1 lemon
450 g (1 lb) young spinach leaves

METHOD: Preheat the oven to gas mark 6/400°F/200°C.

Melt the butter in a small saucepan, whisk in the flour and milk and cook until boiling over a moderate heat. Reduce the heat and continue cooking for 5 minutes, making sure the mixture does not colour. Remove from the heat, stir in the egg yolks and the cheese, season with salt and pepper and add a pinch of cayenne pepper.

Butter a 1 litre (2 pint) soufflé dish, line with buttered greaseproof paper slightly proud of the top and dust with breadcrumbs. Whisk the egg whites stiffly and fold in the cheese mixture gently. Spoon into the soufflé dish and bake for 25–30 minutes or until set.

Finely chop the sun-dried tomatoes, stir in 110 ml (4 fl oz) of olive oil and the juice from the lemon. Toss the salad leaves in this mixture and arrange on 4 plates, spoon over the soufflé and serve.

If you wish you can twice-bake the soufflé in individual ramekins. To do this halve the mixture and use size-two ramekins, about 8 cm (3¼ inch) in diameter. They will cook in about 15 minutes. Allow to cool slightly, gently remove with a spatula. Later on when you are ready to eat you return them to a hot oven on a metal tray for 5 minutes so they puff up again. Serve on the salad as before.

GOAT'S CHEESE, SPINACH AND RED PEPPER TERRINE

Some years ago I took a deep breath and splashed out on an expensive cast-iron terrine pot with a lid. I have always enjoyed making terrines, whether with meat, vegetables or fish, and for years I had struggled with a bread tin and foil. There is nothing wrong with the latter, but part of the joy of making terrines now is taking down this weighty piece of equipment.

MAKES ONE TERRINE

4 red peppers	*bunch fresh basil*
700 g (1½ lb) spinach	*olive oil*
225 g (8 oz) goat's cheese	*2 tablespoons chopped parsley*
salt and pepper	*3 lemons, halved*

METHOD: Preheat the oven to gas mark 6/400°F/200°C and roast the red peppers until the skin goes black – they need to be turned once or twice and take about 20 minutes. Remove from the oven and put in a bowl, cover with cling film and set aside for 10 minutes. Peel and deseed the peppers when cool enough to handle. If you are in a hurry do this under cold running water to save your fingers from burning.

Blanch the spinach in boiling salted water for 2 minutes, refresh under cold water and allow to drain. Squeeze out any excess moisture and pat dry with kitchen paper. Cut the goat's cheese into thin slices.

Line a terrine dish with cling film and arrange a layer of spinach in the bottom. Season with salt and pepper, follow with a layer of basil leaves, cheese and then a layer of red pepper, seasoning each layer as you go. Continue until you use up all the ingredients.

Pour over 110 ml (4 fl oz) of olive oil, wrap the cling film round the ingredients tightly and weigh down – tins of tomatoes are useful for this. Put in the fridge overnight. To serve, slice the terrine, remove the cling film from each slice, arrange on a plate, sprinkle over the parsley and serve with a lemon half.

Baked chicory with
pancetta and parmesan

Pancetta is exactly the same cut of pork as bacon – the belly, a succulent mixture of lean and fat that is cured for around 20 days. There are two types of pancetta, stesa (which you want for this recipe) and arrotolata, which is rolled and flavoured, sometimes with cloves and pepper and sometimes smoked. It also tends to be a bit leaner. You can substitute bacon for the pancetta, but it is well worth seeking out the Italian variety, which apart from crisping up more easily, also tastes sweeter.

SERVES 4

8 heads of chicory	*nutmeg*
salt and pepper	*50 g (2 oz) freshly grated Parmesan*
50 g (2 oz) pancetta	*50 g (2 oz) breadcrumbs*
110 g (4 oz) butter	

METHOD: Preheat the oven to gas mark 4/350°F/180°C.

Blanch the chicory in boiling salted water for 5 minutes, drain, refresh under cold water, pat dry and slice in half lengthways. Arrange, cut-side up, in a shallow earthenware dish. Cut the pancetta into bite-sized pieces and sauté over a gentle heat in the butter until just crisp. Scatter the pancetta over the chicory and pour over the butter.

Season with salt and pepper and grate over a little nutmeg. Combine the Parmesan and breadcrumbs, sprinkle over the chicory and bake for 25 minutes, or until brown and bubbling.

COURGETTE FRITTERS WITH
CHERRY TOMATO SALAD

Our tradition of meat and two veg strips too many vegetables of their true glory. Nowhere is this more true than with courgettes. Somehow they get lost when served up with other vegetables and meat and yet on their own they have a truly regal quality, the Mediterranean at its best.

SERVES 4

225 g (½ lb) cherry tomatoes
4 spring onions, finely chopped
olive oil
salt and pepper
2 dessertspoons chopped tarragon

110 g (4 oz) flour
1 teaspoon baking powder
1 egg
pinch of ground cinnamon
8 courgettes (about 225 g/½ lb)

METHOD: Roughly chop the tomatoes and mix with the spring onions, 5 tablespoons of olive oil, a seasoning of salt and pepper and the tarragon. Set aside.

Combine the flour, baking powder, egg, cinnamon and 4 tablespoons of cold water. Whisk until you have a smooth batter (you may need to add more water). Trim the courgettes and cut lengthways into about ½ cm (¼ inch) thick slices. Dip in the batter and deep-fry in 2.5 cm (1 inch) of olive oil, heated until just before it starts to smoke, until golden.

Drain on kitchen paper and serve on top of a generous spoonful of the tomato salad.

COURGETTES
MARINATED WITH PECORINO

Popular throughout central and southern Italy, Pecorino is made from ewe's milk and comes in various sizes, shapes and textures depending on how long it has been aged. Romano is the strongest, at eight months, and Pecorino Siciliano at the other extreme can be eaten the day after it is made. It is a delightful cheese, with a whole range of tastes. For this recipe you need to find one that is at least a few months old.

SERVES 4

6 courgettes
1 garlic clove, peeled and finely chopped
110 ml (4 fl oz) olive oil
handful of parsley

handful of basil leaves
1 lemon
110 g (4 oz) Pecorino
salt and pepper

METHOD: Preheat the grill. Trim the courgettes and slice lengthways, each strip about ½ cm (¼ inch) thick. Grill until slightly charred. Remove from the grill, place in a bowl, add the garlic and pour over the olive oil.

Roughly chop all the parsley and basil and add these to the courgettes along with the zest and juice of the lemon. With a vegetable peeler, cut shavings from the cheese and sprinkle over the courgettes. Season well with salt and pepper and refrigerate for a few hours – the longer the better.

Serve with bread and chilled white wine.

FRENCH BEAN, PEA AND RED ONION STEW WITH GOAT'S CHEESE

In Portugal they dip green beans in batter and then deep-fry them so they look like whitebait – little fish from the garden. These days we have year-round beans jetted in from Kenya and other far-flung gardens, but in the summer it is worth hunting out the home-grown examples, which seem to be sweeter and have more flavour. The peas should be from a pod, not a packet, as the whole point is lost in the freezing process. The sweetness is one thing, but you need the fresh variety to give that deep summer greenness that is an essential part of the pea.

SERVES 4

225 g (½ lb) French beans, trimmed
salt and pepper
olive oil
4 red onions, peeled and cut into
*   half-moon slices*
2 garlic cloves, peeled and finely
*   chopped*
ground cinnamon

225 g (½ lb) shelled peas
1 × 400 g (14 oz) tin chopped
*   tomatoes*
glass of white wine
bunch of fresh basil
110 g (4 oz) goat's cheese, cut into
*   cubes*

METHOD: Blanch the beans in plenty of salted water for 2 minutes, drain and refresh under cold water. Heat 4 tablespoons of olive oil in a saucepan and sauté the onions for 5 minutes. Add the garlic and cinnamon and continue cooking for 2 minutes. Add the peas, tomatoes and wine and simmer for 15 minutes, or until reduced to quite a thick sauce. Stir in the beans and when heated through, add the basil.

Sprinkle the goat's cheese on top and serve with some plain rice or boiled potatoes. You can also serve this in smaller portions as a first course.

BAKED MUSHROOMS WITH GOAT'S CHEESE
AND TOMATOES

I adore wild mushrooms, but almost equally the large flat field mushrooms with their dark, forbidding gills. Years ago, before we got so keen on covering the land with fertiliser, I used to walk through the fields of my grandmother's small farm in the West of Ireland and pick them for breakfast. Collecting the eggs on the way through the yard was a bonus, but nothing compared to the fresh soda bread that would appear out of the Aga and the yellow butter that would come up from the dairy underneath the kitchen. I am more likely to eat this recipe on a Sunday evening, but it's that memory which prompted the idea.

SERVES 4

25 g (1 oz) dried porcini (available from some supermarkets and from most Italian delicatessens)
450 g (1 lb) large flat mushrooms
2 onions, peeled and finely chopped
olive oil
2 garlic cloves, peeled and finely chopped

225 g (½ lb) medium-strength goat's cheese, thinly sliced
225 g (½ lb) tomatoes, sliced
salt and pepper
bunch of fresh thyme
225 ml (8 fl oz) passata (bottled sieved tomatoes)
110 g (4 oz) freshly grated Parmesan

METHOD: Soak the porcini in warm water and set aside. Wipe the fresh mushrooms clean – avoid water, mushrooms don't like it. Cut into roughly equal sizes and set aside. Sauté the onion in 5 tablespoons of olive oil for 10 minutes without colouring. Add the mushrooms and porcini (drained of their liquid, which should be reserved) and continue cooking until the mushrooms just start to release their juices (about 5 minutes). Stir in the garlic and set aside.

Preheat the oven to gas mark 4/350°F/180°C. In a shallow gratin dish alternate layers of mushrooms, goat's cheese and sliced tomatoes, seasoning as you go and sprinkling over a generous quantity of thyme. Mix the passata with the reserved porcini liquid (taking care to leave the grit behind) and pour over the dish. Sprinkle the Parmesan on top and bake for 30 minutes, or until golden and bubbling.

MUSHROOM, TALEGGIO AND SPINACH BRUSCHETTA

Talaggio should come from Lombardy, where its production is controlled by law. Traditionally made in eight-inch squares, it is soft, with a reddish skin that has a slightly gritty texture. The whole cheese has a salty tang to it, having matured for two to three months in caves in the Alps. More mature versions are slightly stronger, with a delightful creamy texture. If you care to eat the cheese uncooked, try it with quince cheese, or a fruity preserve.

SERVES 4

4 slices of good quality country bread
olive oil
2 garlic cloves, peeled
2 tablespoons finely chopped shallots
450 g (1 lb) mushrooms

25 g (1 oz) dried porcini reconstituted
in 110 ml (4 fl oz) hot water
225 g (½ lb) spinach
110 g (4 oz) taleggio

METHOD: Lightly brush the bread with olive oil and grill until golden brown. Slice one of the garlic cloves in half and rub into the grilled bread and set aside. Finely chop all the garlic.

Lightly sauté the shallots in 2 tablespoons of olive oil for 10 minutes without colouring. Roughly chop the mushrooms and add to the shallots. Sauté, stirring frequently, for 5 minutes, or until the mushrooms yield their juices. Add the garlic and continue frying for 2 minutes. Stir in the soaked porcini, along with the liquid, taking care to hold back the grit at the end. Add the spinach and continue to cook for a further 2 minutes. Remove from the heat, slice the taleggio and stir into the mushrooms. Serve on top of the bread with a generous seasoning of salt and pepper.

OKRA WITH FRESH TOMATO
AND BASIL SAUCE

I was first introduced to okra as bindi, the ingredient in one of the most refreshing curries I have ever eaten. At a petrol station outside the central Indian city of Kanpur around midnight I scooped up this thick, slightly crunchy curry in wedges of bread and somehow knew it must be the first authentic Indian food I had ever eaten: earthy, spicy, fragrant and so fresh tasting. Okra, otherwise known as lady's fingers, originate from America, where they are the essential ingredient of gumbo.

SERVES 4

1 onion, peeled and finely chopped
olive oil
700 g (1½ lb) okra, washed and
*   trimmed*
2 carrots, peeled and finely chopped
50 g (2 oz) pancetta, chopped finely
1 tablespoon chopped parsley

2 garlic cloves, peeled and finely
*   chopped*
900 g (2 lb) tomatoes
1 glass white wine
salt and pepper
bunch of basil, roughly chopped

METHOD: Soften the onion in 3 tablespoons of olive oil for 15 minutes without colouring. Add the okra, carrot, pancetta, parsley and garlic and continue cooking for 5 minutes over a low heat.

Drop the tomatoes into boiling water for 20 seconds, refresh under cold water, peel, deseed and finely chop. Add to the okra along with the white wine and a seasoning of salt and pepper. Cook, uncovered, over a moderate heat for 25 minutes. Stir in the basil at the last minute and serve with rice.

ROAST PEPPERS AND
CHICKPEA STEW

Chickpeas have been around for as long as anyone can remember, being a staple food in India and Asia, from where they spread around the Mediterranean and up through France. Full of carbohydrates, proteins and minerals, they are a wonderful pulse, with bags of nutty flavour and a surprisingly creamy texture. Cicero is supposed to have derived his name from a chickpea-like wart that sat rather predominantly on the end of some relative's nose. Old Mr Chickpea may have been called that as a joke, but the name stuck.

SERVES 2

1 onion, peeled and finely chopped
olive oil
6 carrots, peeled and quartered
lengthways
2 garlic cloves, crushed (you can leave
the skin on)
1 × 400 g (14 oz) tin of chickpeas, or
the same weight of dried chickpeas

soaked overnight and cooked in
boiling water
cayenne pepper
570 ml (1 pint) chicken or vegetable
stock
salt and pepper
2 red peppers
225 g (8 oz) mangetout

METHOD: Sauté the onion in 2 tablespoons of olive oil for 10 minutes, without colouring. Add the carrots and garlic and continue to cook for 5 minutes. Add the chickpeas, a pinch of cayenne pepper and the stock. Season with salt and pepper, slowly bring to the boil and simmer for 30 minutes.

Blacken the peppers under a hot, preheated grill and when the skin is all fairly charred transfer to a bowl and cover with cling film for 10 minutes. Remove the cling film and allow to cool, then peel.

Finely slice the mangetout lengthways and toss briefly in a hot frying pan with a little olive oil, salt and pepper – 3 minutes at the most. Serve the mangetout on top of the chickpeas with the grilled peppers layered on top of everything.

WHOLE ROASTED PEPPERS WITH
ANCHOVY STUFFING AND
FENNEL SALAD

The first time I roasted a pepper I couldn't believe the metamorphosis that took place. Grill or roast the skins till they go black and papery, allow to cool and remove, and this essentially crunchy, slightly bitter hot vegetable becomes sublimely moist, sweet and succulent with a richness that is at once velvety without being sickly. Mix the red and yellow varieties with anchovies and capers, dress with olive oil, lemon juice and fresh basil leaves and you have one of the most impressive and colourful starters. This recipe is adapted from an antipasta dish I had in Sardinia some years ago.

SERVES 4

4 red peppers	*225 g (8 oz) ricotta*
4 fennel bulbs	*110 g (4 oz) white anchovies*
olive oil	*(available from Italian*
salt and pepper	*delicatessens), roughly chopped*
2 lemons	*2 tablespoons chopped parsley*

METHOD: In a hot oven, or under the grill, cook the peppers until the skins go black; you'll need to turn them two or three times. Remove to a bowl and cover with cling film or a damp tea towel.

Trim the fennel bulbs top and bottom, place the bulb root-end down on a chopping board and slice thinly. Blanch in boiling water for 3 minutes and refresh under cold water. Toss with 5 tablespoons of olive oil, salt and pepper and the juice of 1 lemon; set aside.

Push the ricotta through a sieve using a wooden spoon and combine with the anchovies and parsley. Whisk in the juice of the remaining lemon, stirring and tasting as you go – you may not need all the lemon juice. Season with salt and pepper.

Peel the peppers and remove the core, taking care not to tear the flesh. Fill each pepper with a quarter of the filling and refrigerate for at least 20 minutes, longer if possible. Arrange on top of the fennel and serve. Stuffing the peppers is somewhat messy, but don't worry if a little of the mixture oozes out – it will set in the fridge.

Potato cakes with sour cream,
chives and leek salad

Becoming too attached to potatoes can be a dangerous thing, as we Irish found to our cost during the Famine. But it's hard not to; partnered with rivers of slowly melting butter and a generous sprinkling of salt and pepper, or baked with any number of toppings, it is a vegetable fit for any king or queen. At least Marie Antoinette thought so – when Parmentier presented Louis XIV with a bunch of potato flowers she was so charmed with them she placed one in her hair, thus ensuring the court's acceptance of the humble spud.

SERVES 6

12 young leeks, trimmed and washed *450 g (1 lb) floury potatoes (Kerrs*
salt and pepper *Pink, King Edward or Maris*
olive oil *Piper, for example)*
lemon juice *50 g (2 oz) butter*
bunch of chives *2 eggs, separated*
275 ml (½ pint) soured cream *50 g (2 oz) plain flour*

METHOD: Blanch the leeks in boiling salted water for 3 minutes, drain and refresh under cold water. Pat dry, toss in olive oil and cook under a preheated grill for 5 minutes, turning so the surface of the leeks just begin to char. Squeeze over a little lemon juice and set aside.

Chop the chives as finely as you possibly can and mix with the cream, set aside. Peel the potatoes and cook until tender. While still hot, mash and stir in the butter, a generous seasoning of salt and pepper and the egg yolks. Sift in the flour, stirring all the time. Stiffly whisk the egg whites and fold in the potato mixture.

Lightly oil a frying pan and cook the potato pancake until brown. Place a plate over the top of the frying pan and carefully turn it over. Slide the inverted pancake back into the pan and brown on the other side. Cut into 6 triangles and serve with the leeks and soured cream.

SAUTÉED POTATOES WITH ROSEMARY

Nestling alongside the mighty Rhône, south of Lyon, squeezed between railways and roads heading south and north, is the small village of Ampuis, home to some of the greatest names in winemaking. On one visit I had lunch in the home of a local artist which consisted of this dish, some bread, a salad and cheese. I have had it many times since. It places the potato in its rightful central position and makes use of one of my favourite herbs, rosemary. For authenticity, the whole frying pan – preferably of the heavy iron variety, with a long handle – should be brought to the table. Bowl scrapers, of which I am a self-confessed leader, should be encouraged.

SERVES 4

900 g (2 lb) potatoes, washed but with   3 garlic cloves, unpeeled
skins on   salt and pepper
goose fat (or olive oil)   1 dessertspoon finely chopped rosemary

METHOD: Cut the potatoes into cubes about the same size as a dice. Heat 5 tablespoons of goose fat in a large frying pan and when hot slide in the potatoes and garlic. Allow to cook in the hot fat for 3 minutes and then start to toss them gently. Carry on cooking them for 15–20 minutes, until golden brown. Adjust the heat so the fat doesn't burn and the potatoes cook evenly. Don't allow the temperature to fall too low, however, or the result will taste greasy.

Remove the garlic, season with salt and pepper, sprinkle over the rosemary, toss well, and bring the whole pan to the table.

GRILLED POTATOES WITH MIXED MUSHROOMS AND WATERCRESS SALAD

Availability of potatoes has improved enormously, with main supermarkets now supplying a range to choose from. The next step will be for them to stop labelling them as being suitable for roasting or boiling and tell us what they actually are. For preference, I like to buy my potatoes with a little mud adhering to the skin – that way they retain rather more flavour.

SERVES 4

450 g (1 lb) cooked salad potatoes (e.g. Pink Fir Apple, Charlotte or Jersey Royals)
110 g (4 oz) each of open flat mushrooms, oyster and shitake
olive oil
salt and pepper

1 garlic clove, peeled and finely chopped
2 handfuls of basil leaves
1 tablespoon pine nuts
1 dessertspoon grated Parmesan
4 handfuls of watercress
1 tablespoon chopped parsley

METHOD: Cut the potatoes in half and put in a roasting tin along with the mushrooms. Pour over 5 tablespoons of olive oil and toss the vegetables so they are well coated. Season the lot with salt and pepper and put under a preheated grill, turning once, until the mushrooms are cooked – about 10–15 minutes.

In a liquidiser or food processor blend the garlic, basil leaves, pine nuts and Parmesan with 110 ml (4 fl oz) of olive oil. Season with salt and pepper and set aside.

Put the watercress on 4 plates, distribute the potatoes and mushrooms on top and ladle over the basil oil. Sprinkle over the chopped parsley and serve.

WARM POTATO AND SPINACH SALAD WITH HERB AND ANCHOVY DRESSING

There has been a huge resurgence of interest in some of the older varieties of potato, particularly salad potatoes like Ratte, Pink Fir Apple, Kipfler or the mysterious Purple Congo, its dark skin and flesh hiding a light, nutty flavour. All are suitable for this recipe and certainly the first three I have seen on sale in supermarkets. I used to eat potatoes all the time but now only do so occasionally, which somehow makes them more delicious and even more of a treat than before. This salad, followed by some farmhouse cheese, is a favourite mid-week treat of mine.

SERVES 4

900 g (2 lb) new potatoes
salt and pepper
6 anchovies (the pale, loose-packed
*   variety available from Italian*
*   delicatessens)*

olive oil
1 lemon
225 g (½ lb) baby spinach
1 dessertspoon each of chopped sage,
*   thyme and parsley*

METHOD: Steam or boil the potatoes in salted water until tender, about 10–15 minutes. Drain and leave in the saucepan, covered with a tea towel. In a large bowl mash the anchovies with the back of a wooden spoon and whisk in 110 ml (4 fl oz) of olive oil. Add lemon juice to taste and then the spinach and herbs.

Cut the potatoes in half and add to the spinach. Toss the whole assembly well, season with salt and pepper and serve.

GRILLED RADICCHIO WITH BRIOCHE AND MUSHROOMS

For years I have been enjoying radicchio in salads, its speckled mauve colouring and slightly bitter taste a foil for some of the paler, sweeter salad leaves. Then I read Anna Del Conte's *Entertaining all'Italiana* where, in one of the menus, radicchio (*radiko* in Italian) is grilled along with chicory. This is a delight: a sweetness is drawn out and if your radicchio is good, it is partnered by exactly the right sour note from the wilted leaves. I have just used radicchio in this recipe, but you could add chicory for more variety if you wish. Brioche is sold in most supermarkets in the form of individual cakes, often pre-wrapped.

SERVES 4

1 head of radicchio
olive oil
salt and pepper
450 g (1 lb) assorted mushrooms

4 brioche cakes, cut in thirds
4 handfuls assorted salad leaves
1 lemon

METHOD: Trim the core and any discoloured leaves from the radicchio and then cut into 6 so that each wedge is held together by a little of the core at the bottom. Arrange in a frying pan and dribble over 4 tablespoons of olive oil and a generous seasoning of salt and pepper. Set aside.

Wipe the mushrooms clean and cut into equal sizes. Preheat the grill, toast the brioche and set aside. Grill the radicchio in the frying pan placed under the heat until the leaves soften and are slightly charred. Remove from the pan and keep warm. Over a high heat fry the mushrooms in the same pan, adding a little more oil if necessary, until they yield up their juices. Season with salt and pepper.

Lightly dress the salad leaves with olive oil and lemon juice, arrange on 4 plates, distribute the radicchio and top with the brioche and mushrooms.

STUFFED RADICCHIO WITH
MANGETOUT AND SPINACH SALAD

The radicchio we most often see, with its familiar dusty pink leaves, is just one of the three varieties of radicchio available in Italy. What we know as radicchio was only developed after the last war and is generally considered the inferior one, the others having a more delicate, sweeter flavour. Inferior it may be, but I still find it delicious.

SERVES 4

4 small radicchio
225 g (½ lb) mangetout
4 handfuls of spinach leaves
110 g (4 oz) shelled walnuts, roughly
  chopped

225 g (8 oz) ricotta
2 tablespoons chopped parsley
1 dessertspoon chopped thyme
salt and pepper
olive oil

METHOD: Preheat the oven to gas mark 4/350°F/180°C.

Blanch the radicchio in boiling salted water for 2 minutes, refresh under cold water and drain. Trim the core of any brown bits, but leave the bulk of it so the leaves are still attached. Peel away as many of the outside leaves as you can and cut out the central core with a sharp knife. Roughly chop this core and put in a bowl along with the mangetout, which should be very finely chopped lengthways, and the spinach.

In a separate bowl, combine the walnuts, ricotta, parsley and thyme and mix well. Season with salt and pepper and stuff the radicchio, drawing the leaves up round the stuffing – don't worry if the ricotta shows at the top a bit. Dribble a little olive oil over each radicchio and bake for 20 minutes.

Toss the spinach, mangetout and radicchio leaves with a little olive oil, season with salt and pepper and serve the stuffed radicchio on top.

RATATOUILLE

With many popular dishes, familiarity often shrouds the original concept behind the recipe and destroys all its subtlety and grace. This has been the fate of ratatouille. Its decline into a vegetable stew, the components hurled carelessly into a pot, has blocked out all the colour and abundance this regional speciality of Provence is meant to convey. Yet the bright, thick richness of aubergines, the sublime sweetness of peppers, the piquant focus of tomatoes, all bound together with the heady aroma of herbs and olive oil, is surely one of the most wonderful combinations. Hot, cold; with lamb, grilled meats or sausages; simply with rice, or with potatoes or beans, it is heaven. The vegetables should be cooked separately and then combined towards the end. Traditionally they were fried in olive oil, but I find the end result lighter if they are grilled first and then combined.

SERVES 6 AS A MAIN COURSE

3 onions, peeled and finely chopped
3 red peppers
450 g (1 lb) aubergine
450 g (1 lb) courgettes
olive oil

450 g (1 lb) tomatoes
2 garlic cloves, peeled and chopped
½ teaspoon coriander seeds, roughly
*   crushed*
large bunch of basil

METHOD: Gently sauté the onions in 110 ml (4 fl oz) of olive oil for 15 minutes without colouring. Heat the grill – if you have a ridged griddle pan, so much the better – and cook the peppers until the skin goes black. Transfer to a bowl, cover with cling film and set aside. Cut the aubergines into discs about ½ cm (¼ inch) thick and the courgettes into strips slightly thinner. Lightly brush with olive oil and grill until brown on both sides.

Drop the tomatoes into boiling water for 30 seconds, refresh under cold water, skin and deseed. When the peppers are cool enough to handle, remove the skin and the seeds and tear into strips.

Add the garlic and coriander to the onions, turn the heat up slightly and sauté for 2 minutes. Add the peppers, tomatoes, courgettes and aubergines and gently stir. Lower the heat and cook for 30 minutes, making sure nothing catches on the bottom. Remove from the heat, stir in the basil and serve.

RED ONION TARTE TATIN

Root vegetables have a natural sweetness that works well in tarts and this version has the added bonus of a dramatic colour that comes from the caramelised sugar mixing with the red onions. The credit for inventing tarte Tatin is generally given to the Tatin sisters who were apparently trying to invent a way of ensuring crispy pastry. I'm still amused by the story every time I make the dish, imagining them pondering over this great problem and then suddenly resolving it with such a simple solution – cook the thing upside down. No matter how charming (or authentic) this story might be, this upside-down tart was and is popular throughout Orléanais.

MAKES ONE 25 CM (10 INCH) TART

700 g (1½ lb) red onions, peeled and
halved
caster sugar
2 garlic cloves

1 heaped teaspoon chopped rosemary
salt and pepper
225 g (8 oz) shortcrust pastry

METHOD: Preheat the oven to gas mark 6/400°F/200°C.

Place the onions in an ovenproof frying pan with a heaped teaspoon of sugar on top of each one. Bake for 20 minutes, remove and allow to cool slightly.

Put 50 g (2 oz) of caster sugar in the pan and caramelise over a moderate heat until dark, but not burned – if it burns, you'll need to start again. Remove from the heat, put one half-onion cut-side up in the middle and arrange the remaining onions, quartered, around it. Sprinkle over the garlic and rosemary and season with salt and pepper. Roll out the pastry and place on top of the onions, tucking the edges in. Bake for 25 minutes, or until brown. Rest for 10 minutes, turn on to a plate and serve.

ROAST MEDITERRANEAN VEGETABLES WITH POLENTA AND BLACK OLIVE DRESSING

This is a favourite, labour-free recipe, particularly suited to the end of summer, when courgettes and tomatoes are plentiful and the cook is exhausted. Into the bottom of a hot oven goes the polenta, into the top go the vegetables, and you are free to spend the next 45 minutes as you wish while the kitchen is filled with the gentle smell of caramelising vegetables. You can buy 'instant' polenta, which can be made in minutes, but that is not what is intended here. If you wish to use the instant variety, follow the instructions on the packet and roast the vegetables as described.

SERVES 6

275 g (10 oz) polenta　　　　　*salt and pepper*
4 medium courgettes　　　　　*3 red peppers*
*　　(about 450 g/1 lb)*　　　　*glass of white wine*
2 large aubergines　　　　　*4 roughly chopped tomatoes*
3 red onions, peeled　　　　　*bunch of thyme*
olive oil　　　　　　　　　*110 g (4 oz) pitted black olives*
2 garlic cloves, finely chopped　*1 lemon*

METHOD: Preheat the oven to gas mark 4/350°F/180°C.

Bring 3 pints of water to the boil with 2 teaspoons of salt. Add the polenta in a steady stream, stirring all the time, and then pour into a roasting tin. Put in the bottom of the oven for 1 hour.

Roughly chop the courgettes, aubergines and red onions and toss in a little olive oil and the garlic. Season with salt and pepper and place in a roasting tin. Wash the peppers and place these at the side of the tin. Put the whole lot at the top of the oven and roast for 45 minutes. Remove the peppers to a covered bowl after 20 minutes. Peel and deseed the peppers, under cold water if they are too hot.

Add the white wine and tomatoes to the roasting tin and scrape up all the caramelised bits at the bottom over a moderate heat. Stir in a generous sprinkling of thyme and the peeled peppers. Combine the olives with 110 ml (4 fl oz) of olive oil and lemon juice to taste. Serve the vegetables with a generous helping of polenta and the black olive dressing dribbled over the top.

ROOT VEGETABLE GRATIN DAUPHINOIS

The first time I ate gratin dauphinois I really thought I would die a happy man. The potato dish was served, as a course of its own, at the end of a long and heavy meal. I had just reached that stage where I thought, 'no more, this is enough,' and my host put this dish in the middle of the table. Spirits were revived, the chat flowed, and we ate the entire thing, right down to the crispy bits on the sides of the dish. Dauphinois refers to a region in France extending from Savoy down to Provence, so varied it seems pointless to talk about specialities. However, the quality of its milk and cream has always been recognised, hence the famous gratin. There are versions that include eggs and cheese, but this seems to me to take away from the celebration of garlic and cream. The flour is there to stop the cream separating.

SERVES 4

225 g (½ lb) potatoes	*salt and pepper*
225 g (½ lb) turnips	*3 garlic cloves, peeled and finely*
225 g (½ lb) Jerusalem artichokes	*chopped*
225 g (½ lb) parsnips	*570 ml (1 pint) single cream*
butter	*1 teaspoon plain flour*

METHOD: Preheat the oven to gas mark 6/400°F/200°C.

Peel and thinly slice the vegetables; a mandolin or the thin blade of a food processor give the most consistent results. Blanch in boiling water for 2 minutes. Remove, refresh under cold water and pat dry.

Lightly butter a gratin dish and scatter in the vegetables, seasoning with salt and pepper as you go and a sprinkling of garlic. Mix the cream and flour and pour over the vegetables. Cover with tin foil and bake for 1 hour, removing the tin foil and turning the heat up as high as it will go for the last 10 minutes. This dish will sit quite happily in a warm oven for up to an hour.

SOURDOUGH BRUSCHETTA
WITH BABA GHANOUSH
AND WILTED SPINACH

There seem to be as many recipes for baba ghanoush as there are spellings of the name. Some incorporate yoghurt, others tomatoes, some use both, although purists do not approve of combining yoghurt and tahini in the same dish. Keep it simple is my motto. Sourdough bread, made over several days using the natural yeasts that exist in flour, has a density and texture quite unlike any other. You can find it in delicatessens, but if it is difficult to come by any good quality bread will suffice. I generally use this as a first course, but it also makes a wonderfully indulgent vegetarian supper for two.

SERVES 6 AS A FIRST COURSE

2 medium-sized aubergines
450 g (1 lb) spinach
2 garlic cloves, peeled
2 tablespoons tahini (available in most
supermarkets)
juice of 1 lemon

1 tablespoon finely chopped parsley
1 tablespoon coriander leaves
olive oil
salt and pepper
6 large slices sourdough bread, brushed
with olive oil and grilled

METHOD: Preheat the oven to gas mark 5/375°F/190°C.

Prick the skins of the aubergines with a carving fork and bake in the oven for 30 minutes, or until the flesh is soft. Remove and allow to cool so you can handle them without burning your hands. Cut in half and scoop out the flesh into a bowl. Mash with a fork. You may prefer to use a food processor, but I like the rough finish achieved with a fork.

Blanch the spinach in boiling water for 30 seconds, refresh under cold water and gently squeeze out the excess water. Don't squeeze too hard, though, or you'll squash the leaves.

Crush the garlic cloves with a hard blow from your hand on the back of a large sharp knife and then chop the pulp finely. Add this, along with the tahini, lemon juice, parsley and coriander to the aubergine. Stir everything thoroughly, and add enough olive oil to give a thick rich consistency. Season with salt and pepper, spread the spinach on the bread, top with the baba ghanoush and serve.

RICOTTA AND SPINACH PANCAKES

I wish I ate pancakes more often. Easy to make from inexpensive store-cupboard ingredients, they make a delightful feast when served simply with lemon juice and sugar and take on a whole different dimension when stuffed and baked. Chicken, ham, leftover lamb or beef, whatever vegetables are to hand, the list is endless, although this one with ricotta is my favourite. Ricotta, meaning recooked – literally the reheated whey which has been separated from the curd – must be bought very fresh. It has a tangy sweetness which is deliciously light.

SERVES 4

175 g (6 oz) plain flour　　　　　*450 g (1 lb) spinach*
salt and pepper　　　　　　　　*450 g (1 lb) Ricotta*
850 ml (1½ pints) milk　　　　*nutmeg*
2 eggs　　　　　　　　　　　*1 × 400 g (14 oz) tin of strained*
110 g (4 oz) unsalted butter　　　　*chopped tomatoes*
110 ml (4 fl oz) white wine　　　*4 tablespoons Parmesan*

METHOD: Sift 110 g (4 oz) of the plain flour into a bowl and add a generous pinch of salt. Whisk in 275 ml (½ pint) of the milk and then add the eggs and 50 g (2 oz) of the butter, melted (use the frying pan you will make the pancakes in to save on washing up). Lightly grease the frying pan – the pancakes shouldn't fry – then pour in a light coating of the batter and when set, flip them by throwing the frying pan forward and then jerking your wrist so the pan moves upwards. It usually takes two or three goes to get into the swing at first.

Meanwhile make a sauce by melting the remaining butter in a saucepan and stirring in the remaining flour. Cook for 2 minutes without browning and then add the remaining milk and white wine. Cook until it thickens – about 5 minutes.

Preheat the oven to gas mark 5/375°F/190°C. Heat the spinach in a covered saucepan over a low heat, tossing frequently until it wilts. Mash the ricotta with a fork and whisk into the spinach. Season well with salt and pepper and nutmeg. Put a generous spoonful of the mixture in each pancake and roll up. Spoon a little of the tomatoes into a gratin dish, lay the pancakes on top and surround with the remaining tomatoes and white sauce. Sprinkle over the Parmesan and cook in the oven for 30 minutes, or until brown and bubbling.

SPINACH, GOAT'S CHEESE AND RED PEPPER TART

Whether spinach is blanched in boiling water, wilted in hot oil or eaten raw in salads, its curiously resilient leaves have a delicate sweetness. In the past this has been put to good use in tarts, prepared when no fruit was available. Combining spinach with goat's cheese is like introducing old friends – the two just know how to get on.

MAKES ONE 23 CM (9 INCH) TART

1 red and 1 yellow pepper
225 g (8 oz) shortcrust pastry
(homemade or frozen)
450 g (1 lb) spinach, washed and
drained
50 g (2 oz) butter

salt and pepper
juice and zest from 1 lemon
110 g (4 oz) goat's cheese, cut into
small cubes
2 dessertspoons pine nuts

METHOD: Preheat the oven to gas mark 4/350°F/180°C.

Place the peppers right at the top and roast until the skins go black, turning once or twice. Remove, put in a bowl, cover with a plate or cling film and leave to steam.

While the peppers are roasting, roll out the pastry and line a 23 cm (9 inch) tart tin. Prick with a fork, loosely cover with tin foil and bake for 30 minutes, or until cooked, on the middle shelf at the same time as the peppers. The tin foil is to stop the pepper juices from falling on the pastry.

Blanch the spinach in boiling water for 30 seconds, drain and refresh under cold water. Gently squeeze out as much water as possible and roughly chop. Return to the saucepan and over a gentle heat stir in the butter. Season with salt and pepper and stir in the lemon juice and zest. Peel, deseed and tear the peppers into strips and combine with the spinach.

Arrange the spinach and peppers in the bottom of the pastry shell. Sprinkle over the goat's cheese and pine nuts. Return to the oven and bake for 15 minutes until just warmed through with the cheese beginning to melt. Serve with lots of lightly dressed salad leaves.

SPRING VEGETABLE TARTS
WITH BASIL OIL

Elizabeth Bourgeois leads the all-female team at Le Mas Tourteron in Provence, the sort of restaurant I always want to find when I'm travelling: a beautiful enclosed garden, lots of shade, the sound of running water and a spectacular view. The food is a delight – full of colour, delicate and well balanced – and her spring tart in particular is spectacular. This is my adaptation of her triumph. Buy the best vegetables you can, and don't skimp on the basil – the dressing should be thick and green. If you are in a hurry, use frozen shortcrust pastry.

SERVES 4

225 g (8 oz) plain flour, sieved
salt and pepper
½ teaspoon ground cumin
110 g (4 oz) softened butter
1 egg
110 g (4 oz) shallots
olive oil
12 baby carrots, peeled

12 asparagus tips
8 sprigs purple sprouting broccoli
4 baby courgettes
1 lemon
generous handful of basil
1 garlic clove, peeled and mashed
salt and pepper

METHOD: Put the flour in a food processor along with a pinch of salt and pepper and the cumin. Add the butter and process until it becomes like breadcrumbs. Add the egg and as soon as it begins to come together, switch off. Wrap in cling film and refrigerate for at least 1 hour. Allow to come back to room temperature, roll out as thinly as possible, line four 10 cm (4 inch) tartlet tins and return to the fridge.

Finely chop the shallots and sauté in 2 tablespoons of olive oil for 10 minutes without colouring. Set aside. Blanch the carrots, asparagus, broccoli and courgettes separately until just cooked, but still al dente. Drain and refresh under cold water.

Combine 110 ml (4 fl oz) of olive oil with a seasoning of salt and pepper and lemon juice to taste. Put in a liquidiser along with the basil leaves and garlic and blitz for 15 seconds. Preheat the oven to gas mark 4/350°F/ 180°C and bake the pastry shells until slightly golden, about 20 minutes. Remove, allow to cool slightly and distribute some of the shallot mixture on the bottom. Arrange the blanched vegetables on top and serve with the basil oil dribbled over the top.

ROAST BUTTERNUT SQUASH WITH
GREEN BEAN AND BLACK OLIVE SALAD

The squash on sale in this country are liable to be a disappointment, since the flesh rarely contains the required sweetness and concentration. A gardening friend recently confided that she picked all her squash in September and squirrelled them away for at least three months. This was the time required for them to lose their moisture and develop any real flavour. Being without a garden, I have found that the only squash I can buy with any confidence is the butternut. They have a bright, sweet flesh that is hard to resist and all the main supermarkets carry them.

SERVES 4

2 butternut squash
olive oil
450 g (1 lb) green beans
salt and pepper

bunch of spring onions
1 lemon
110 g (4 oz) pitted black olives
2 tablespoons finely chopped parsley

METHOD: Preheat the oven to gas mark 5/375°F/190°C.

Peel the squash, cut in half, remove the seeds and chop into 5 cm (2 inch) chunks. Coat the squash in a little oil and roast for 30 minutes, or until tender.

Trim the beans and blanch in salted boiling water for 4 minutes, or until tender. Finely chop the spring onions, including most of the green part. Drain the beans and toss with 5 tablespoons of olive oil, the juice from the lemon, the spring onions and the olives. Sprinkle over the chopped parsley, top with the squash, season with salt and pepper and serve.

STEAMED VEGETABLES WITH BEETROOT DRESSING AND HORSERADISH CREAM

Steaming is one of the quickest ways to cook, and as the heat is intense and moist, there is little danger of the ingredients drying out. Coupled with these advantages, if you steam on top of spices, or some of the more robust herbs, you can infuse their flavour gently into the other ingredients. Try fish on a bed of lemongrass and ginger, for example, or wrap chicken breasts in tarragon leaves and then in cabbage. Not only do they taste delicious, but your kitchen is filled with the most gentle aromas.

SERVES 4

bunch of rosemary
2 bay leaves
4 carrots, trimmed, peeled and cut into
  7.5 cm (3 inch) batons
225 g (½ lb) French beans, trimmed
4 small courgettes, trimmed
1 cucumber, trimmed, deseeded and cut
  into 7.5 cm (3 inch) batons
1 fennel bulb, trimmed and cut
  vertically into thin slices
4 leeks, trimmed and any grit removed

salt and pepper
2 raw beetroots about the size of
  tennis balls
1 lemon
olive oil
2 tablespoons grated horseradish (now
  available in jars from good
  supermarkets)
5 tablespoons double cream
bunch of chives, chopped

METHOD: Put the rosemary and bay leaves on the bottom of the top section of a steamer. Put all the vegetables on top of the herbs, season with salt and pepper and steam for 15 minutes, or until everything is cooked.

Peel, halve and finely slice the beetroot with a vegetable peeler, and mix with the juice from the lemon, 110 ml (4 fl oz) of olive oil and a seasoning of salt and pepper. Combine the grated horseradish with the cream and a seasoning of salt and pepper.

To serve, pile the vegetables on to 4 plates, removing the herbs. Dribble over the beetroot dressing, place a scoop of the horseradish in the middle and sprinkle over the chives.

STIR-FRIED VEGETABLES WITH
SESAME OIL AND CHILLI NOODLES

Much has been written in recent years about the various, indeed multitudinous, varieties of chilli available. Measured on a scale in units similar to the Italian Lire, you can tell what the heat factor will be from a given chilli. Notwithstanding all this guidance, I never seem to have the right chilli and so, most of the time, use a basic, that is unadulterated, chilli sauce. These are available from ethnic supermarkets and have the benefit of consistency. Sesame oil is wonderfully aromatic, but has an infuriatingly low burning point.

SERVES 4

soy sauce
sesame seed oil
2.5 cm (1 inch) piece of ginger, grated
4 spring onions, trimmed and finely
    sliced
225 g (8 oz) thin egg noodles
4 tablespoons of oil for frying
2 leeks, trimmed and cut into thin
    lengths

2 carrots, peeled and cut into thin 5 cm
    (2 inch) batons
2 handfuls of beansprouts
1 small tin bamboo shoots, drained
handful of mangetout, cut lengthways
    into thin strips
chilli sauce

METHOD: Combine 1 dessertspoon of soy sauce with 4 of sesame oil and whisk in the ginger and spring onion. Set aside. Bring a saucepan of water to the boil, drop in the noodles, turn off the heat and leave for 5 minutes or until cooked, then drain and refresh under cold water.

In a wok or deep, heavy frying pan heat the oil until it almost reaches burning point. Add the leeks and carrots and toss in the hot oil for 2 minutes. Add the beansprouts, bamboo shoots and mangetout and continue tossing in the hot oil until the vegetables are just cooked.

Add a dessertspoon of the chilli sauce to the cooked noodles. Serve the noodles and vegetables with the spring onion and ginger dressing.

SUN-DRIED TOMATO MUFFINS WITH
MOZZARELLA AND BASIL PURÉE

You would be hard pushed not to have heard of sun-dried tomatoes, such is our enthusiasm for these wrinkled fruits, traditionally from the southern Italian state of Calabria. They are most commonly sold here in attractive jars, covered with olive oil and proudly displaying a hefty price tag. In Italy, however, many buy them in their dried form – also available here from better Italian delicatessens – reconstitute them and do their own bottling, providing themselves with a relatively inexpensive anti-pasto, a lot more interesting than a packet of crisps and almost as cheap. If you add a little chopped garlic and blitz them in a food processor or liquidiser, they are delicious spread on toast – just the thing to remind you of the Mediterranean sun.

SERVES 4

275 g (10 oz) maize flour (or half
*   maize, half plain)*
3 teaspoons baking powder
salt and pepper
1 egg
275 ml (½ pint) buttermilk
50 g (2 oz) melted butter

175 g (6 oz) sun-dried tomatoes,
*   roughly chopped*
large bunch of fresh basil
olive oil
lemon juice
2 Mozzarella cheeses
4 handfuls of salad leaves

METHOD: Preheat the oven to gas mark 7/425°F/220°C.

Mix the flour, baking powder, half a teaspoon of salt and a seasoning of pepper. Combine the egg, buttermilk and melted butter in a separate bowl. Mix the two together thoroughly and stir in the tomatoes. Spoon the mixture into paper cup-cake holders and bake for 15 minutes or until cooked.

Put the basil leaves, along with 110 ml (4 fl oz) of olive oil, the juice of half a lemon and a seasoning of salt and pepper in a liquidiser and switch on. Add more olive oil as required, and lemon juice to taste.

Slice the Mozzarella and muffins and arrange on top of 4 plates of salad leaves. Dribble over the basil purée and serve.

ITALIAN TOMATO STEW

For this recipe you must have the deepest, reddest, ripest tomatoes you can lay your hands on. You will need all the taste and aroma you can draw out from this wonderful fruit. Heady with the perfume of basil, given grace and power from the porcini mushrooms and the sweeping style of Parmesan, this is my unashamedly Italian celebration of the tomato.

SERVES 4

1.35 kg / (3 lb) tomatoes
2 red onions, peeled and finely chopped
olive oil
2 garlic cloves
bunch of parsley, chopped
50 g (2 oz) dried porcini, reconstituted

in 175 ml (6 fl oz) hot water
salt and pepper
12 slices of French bread
1 large handful of shredded basil
4 tablespoons grated Parmesan

METHOD: Drop the tomatoes into boiling water for 30 seconds, drain, refresh under cold water, skin, quarter and deseed. Gently cook the onions in 3 tablespoons of olive oil for 10 minutes without colouring. Add one of the garlic cloves, peeled and finely chopped, and continue cooking for 2 minutes, then add the parsley.

Remove the porcini from the liquid and add to the onions along with the tomatoes. Add the liquid the porcini have been soaking in, making sure the grit in the bottom of the bowl stays behind. Season well with salt and pepper and simmer for 10 minutes.

Brush the bread with olive oil, grill until golden brown and rub with a cut side of the remaining garlic clove. Stir the basil into the stew, float the bread slices on top and sprinkle over the Parmesan.

TAPENADE CROSTINI WITH PARSLEY SALAD

Tapenade is one of Provence's answers to fast and varied cooking. A heady mixture of capers, anchovies and olives pounded in a mortar with olive oil, lemon juice and a few herbs it perfectly partners meat, fish, eggs and crudities as well as slices of toast. Variations include the addition of garlic, mustard and sometimes a splash of brandy. This recipe is one of my favourites for a light meal; a striking combination of colours and strong flavours that almost transports me to the south of France.

SERVES 6

1 stick of French bread
olive oil
1 garlic clove, cut in half
75 g (3 oz) black olives, stoned
6 anchovy fillets (i.e. 3 anchovies)
2 dessertspoons capers, rinsed in plenty

of cold water and gently squeezed
1 lemon
bunch of flat-leaf parsley
4 handfuls of salad leaves
salt and pepper

METHOD: Preheat the oven to gas mark 6/400°F/200°C.

Cut thin slices of French bread, arrange on a wire rack and brush lightly with olive oil. Put the bread right at the top of the oven. They should take less than 5 minutes to cook – if you can smell them you are too late. Remove from the oven and lightly brush with the cut clove of garlic.

Put the black olives, anchovies and capers into a blender and blitz briefly. Pour in enough olive oil to bind the mixture together, add lemon juice to taste and spread on the crostini. Pick the parsley leaves from the stalks, mix with the salad leaves and dress with salt and pepper, a little olive oil and some lemon juice to taste.

Serve the crostini on top of the salad leaves.

WELSH RABBIT AND WHITE SALAD

Welsh rabbit, Scotch woodcock, devils on horseback – these culinary jokes so popular with the Victorians have rather fallen out of favour. Perhaps their association with long, multi-course feasts has put us off – after all, cheese on toast is not exactly the thing if, satisfied and replete, your thoughts are turning more in the direction of ice-cream, or perhaps something with a little chocolate in it. On the Continent during the nineteenth century, English taverns are supposed to have served up all of these dishes, but as an entrée. Fond as I am of them, they seem a rather heavy way to start or finish anything. Instead, I reserve them for quick, simple suppers.

SERVES 4

50 g (2 oz) butter	*Worcestershire sauce*
1 tablespoon plain flour	*2 fennel bulbs*
150 ml (5 fl oz) milk	*1 head of celery*
175 g (6 oz) strong Cheddar cheese	*juice of 1 lemon*
5 tablespoons ale or stout	*olive oil*
1 dessertspoon Dijon mustard	*salt and pepper*
1 egg	*8 slices good quality bread*

METHOD: Combine the butter, flour and milk in a saucepan and cook over a low heat until it thickens. Continue cooking, without colouring, until the sauce leaves the bottom of the pan cleanly. Add the Cheddar and ale or stout and continue cooking until it starts to bubble. Remove from the heat and whisk in the mustard and egg and add Worcestershire sauce to taste. Allow to cool.

Trim the fennel and celery and slice as thinly as possible; the fennel should be trimmed top and bottom and sliced vertically, the celery trimmed of its outside leaves and sliced crossways. Blanch both vegetables in boiling salted water for 3 minutes, drain and refresh under cold water. Toss in a bowl with the lemon juice, 5 tablespoons of olive oil and a seasoning of salt and pepper.

Preheat the grill, spread the bread with the cheese mixture and grill until brown and bubbling. Serve on top of the white salad.

ZUPPA CUATA
(HIDDEN SOUP)

I first ate this soup in a farmhouse miles up a mountain road in Sardinia, an island that is one of the Mediterranean's best kept secrets. Cut off from most of Europe – charter flights in the summer are the only direct way in – it has remained largely unspoilt. The food is refreshingly simple, the cooking quick and easy. This is the home of Pecorino, which can be eaten both fresh and aged, a sheep's milk cheese which can rival Parmesan. The name of this dish comes from the submerged ingredients which initially are hidden from view.

SERVES 4

1 onion, finely chopped
olive oil
1 garlic clove, peeled and finely chopped
1 × 400 g (14 oz) tin of tomatoes
1 glass of white wine
bunch of thyme, stalks removed

salt and pepper
1 loaf good quality stale bread cut into
  chunks
2 Mozzarella cheeses, sliced
570 ml (1 pint) beef or lamb stock
4 tablespoons grated Pecorino

METHOD: Preheat the oven to gas mark 4/350°F/180°C.

Gently sauté the onion in 2 tablespoons of olive oil for 10 minutes without colouring. Add the garlic, continue cooking for 2 minutes, then add the tomatoes, white wine, thyme and a seasoning of salt and pepper. Add a glass of water and simmer gently for 15 minutes, uncovered.

In a shallow ovenproof dish, arrange the bread and then a layer of the Mozzarella. Pour over the meat stock, top with the tomato sauce and then the Pecorino. Bake for 30–40 minutes.

Fish

Fish is the most sublime of food. From the humble mackerel to the noble sea bass it is amazingly quick to cook and offers some of the most exciting eating: roasted fillets of sole with green beans and black olives, a mountain of broccoli and capers topped with cutlets of poached salmon, or a contrasting assembly of silky smoked haddock with parsley mash – all providing bold colours with bags of flavour.

Fishmongers, whether on the high street or in a supermarket, will deal with all or most of the preparation for you, particularly the removal of the nasty dark bits. Dash home with a couple of plaice, a John Dory or a piece of cod and supper is on the table in minutes. All you need is a little olive oil and wine, a hot oven and a sprinkling of herbs – fresh food at its finest.

Fish needs very little time to cook, but watch for the crucial last few minutes as it will slip from translucent succulence to dry flakiness in seconds. If you are roasting, the skin can be crisped up on fish like cod and John Dory to add to the flavour and offer a contrasting texture. Try experimenting with some of the less common and often inexpensive fish: whole hake is a delight the Spanish know well, but we seem to miss out on; grey mullet is surprisingly fine, with a texture similar to sea bass; conger eel cooks into some of the juiciest steaks. On the subject of eel – when smoked, it loses its sliminess and tastes deliciously meaty.

Shellfish for me means a napkin tucked under the chin and finger food – whether it is mussels, oysters or lobster, although I confess I find the latter almost too rich to eat. I'll sing for cockles and mussels, however, dance for prawns and do almost anything for scallops. Crabs are a favourite and the spider variety are perfect for a long summer evening, although patience is required to extract the most succulent meat.

The following recipes are particular favourites, although with fish, perhaps more than with any other food, you must be guided by availability. Don't go determined to buy Dover sole – if it looks tired it's better to ditch it in favour of what looks good. It's also important to remember that prices fluctuate depending on availability – let the restaurants pay a fortune for sea bass; it may well be cheaper next week.

Freshness, as we all know, is all-important with fish, so where and what do you buy? Fresh, frozen, previously frozen, loose or pre-packed? My own order of preference is fresh from fishermen, fishmongers, wet counters in supermarkets and pre-packs because I think freezing takes some of the sweetness away. But then I'm lucky to have a superb fishmonger at the top of my road. If I lived deep in the countryside, I'd probably say something different.

CAVIAR, CRÈME FRAÎCHE AND POTATO BLINIS

I have only once been lucky enough to eat real caviar in sufficient quantities to decide what all the fuss is about. Armed with nothing but a teaspoon and a glass of champagne, I went forward to do battle with what I was convinced was a load of hype. Within seconds I was defeated, lost in ecstasy, the sheer luxury evident in every glorious mouthful. It seems unfair after this eulogy to mention lumpfish caviar, but I think it stands up rather well. It's convenient, widely sold and will keep quite happily in the door of your fridge. It partners potatoes perfectly, making a wonderfully dramatic dish.

SERVES 4

450 g (1 lb) cooked potatoes
3 eggs, separated
25 g (1 oz) butter
50 ml (2 fl oz) milk
salt and pepper
olive oil

crème fraîche
1 jar black lumpfish caviar
1 jar orange lumpfish caviar
bunch of chives, chopped
2 lemons

METHOD: Mash the potatoes and whisk in the egg yolks, butter and milk to give a sloppy mash (you may need a little more milk). Briskly whisk the egg whites and fold into the mash, seasoning with salt and pepper. Heat a little oil in 4 blini pans and cook a ladle-full of the mixture in each. Turn over and brown the topsides. Transfer to a warm oven once they are cooked.

Top the blinis with a spoonful of crème fraîche and a teaspoon each of the caviar per serving. Sprinkle over the chives and serve with a little salad and a lemon half.

HOME-CURED SALT COD WITH WILTED SPINACH AND AÏOLI

Intense, slightly chewy with a sweet taste and flavour of the sea, salt cod is eaten in France, Spain and Portugal with enthusiasm. Here, however, it is distinctly unpopular. Enforced war-time fodder is one of the offered excuses, an unpalatable saltiness the other. Lack of familiarity probably has a lot to do with it – I've eaten too much delicious brandad in both France and Spain to believe it is the salt cod which is to blame. The salting was traditionally done to preserve the fish so quite a lot was used in the curing. Do it yourself in your fridge and you can use less salt, producing a more subtle, less overpowering result to cook with. You need to do the salting a few days in advance, but once that is completed the dish takes no more time to prepare than it would with unsalted fish.

SERVES 4

900 g (2 lb) thick cod fillet　　*150 ml (5 fl oz) vegetable oil*
salt and pepper　　*1 lemon*
1 garlic clove　　*700 g (1½ lb) spinach*
2 egg yolks　　*plain flour*
150 ml (5 fl oz) olive oil　　*olive oil*

METHOD: Rinse the fish, pat dry and put in an earthenware dish. Sprinkle over 2 tablespoons of sea salt – it must be granular, fine salt will not work – turn the fish and coat well. Cover and put in the fridge for 2 days, turning each day. Rinse the fish under cold water and leave to soak in a bowl of cold water for 2 hours.

My own favoured utensil for making aïoli is a pestle and mortar, the weight of the former making the stirring easier, but a bowl and wooden spoon can be used and, I'm told, a food processor, although I have not tried this last method. The garlic must be pounded to a pulp and then incorporated with the egg yolks. Mix the two oils together – all olive oil makes it too rich in my opinion – and add, drop by drop at first and then in a steady stream. If the sauce splits take a clean bowl, a new egg yolk and gradually add your mixture and then the rest of the oil. Season with lemon juice and salt and pepper at the end to taste.

Blanch the spinach in boiling water for 30 seconds, refresh under cold water and gently squeeze dry. Pat the fish dry and cut into 5 cm (2 inch) or 7.5 cm (3 inch) squares. Season with black pepper and coat in the flour. Fry in olive oil until golden and serve on top of the spinach with the aïoli.

ROAST COD WITH TAPENADE
AND COURGETTE SALAD

Cod, sitting in its pearly white splendour on the fishmonger's slab, holds one of the top places in my list of fish. Cooked *à point*, so the thick flakes of fish can just be prised apart gently with a fork, its delicate sweetness conveys such a subtle hint of the sea. It is one of the most versatile of fish, delicious whether baked, roasted, grilled or fried. The way it is cooked in this recipe allows the skin of the fish to lose that inherent sliminess, so that it is crispy and slightly sour, a perfect contrast to the flesh.

SERVES 4

450 g (1 lb) courgettes
white wine vinegar
salt and pepper
olive oil
75 g (3 oz) black olives, stoned
6 anchovy fillets (i.e. 3 anchovies)

2 dessertspoons capers, rinsed in plenty
*   of cold water and gently squeezed*
3 lemons
bunch of parsley, finely chopped
900 g (2 lb) cod fillet, skin attached,
*   cut into four (try to avoid the tail*
*   end, which will overcook)*

METHOD: Trim and wash the courgettes and then slice lengthways as thinly as possible – a mandolin is the perfect tool for this job, but otherwise a vegetable peeler will do. Combine in a bowl with 1 tablespoon of vinegar, a generous seasoning of salt and pepper and 4 tablespoons of olive oil. Toss and set aside.

Combine the black olives, anchovy fillets and capers and roughly chop. Place in a bowl with the juice from one of the lemons (but taste as you add) and a tablespoon of chopped parsley. Whisk in enough olive oil to form a loose paste and set aside.

Preheat the oven to gas mark 6/400°F/200°C. In a metal-handled frying pan that will fit in the oven, heat 4 tablespoons of olive oil. When almost smoking but not quite, place the fish, seasoned on both sides with salt and pepper, skin-side down in the hot oil. Press lightly down so the skin is in contact with the bottom of the frying pan and fry for 2 minutes without touching. Quickly turn the fish over, transfer to the oven and cook for a further 5 minutes.

Keep the fish warm and lightly toss the courgettes in the frying pan so they are heated through. Arrange on 4 warmed plates and place the cod on top. Put a spoonful of the tapenade on the fish, dribbling a little of the olive oil round the plate, and serve with a quarter lemon each.

FISH SOUP

Fish soups come in many forms and sizes, but for me fish soup is a bowl full of surprises. If possible each mouthful should consist of a different fish, the whole lot suspended in a gloriously rich broth reminiscent of the clean pure smell of sea grass and sand dunes, of the roaring waves of an angry Atlantic. Flat soup plates help enormously – that way you can see what's going on and save the best bits till the end. Variety is essential and if you have a good fishmonger he will endeavour to cut the right number of portions for the number of diners. Trouble is, when you come to serve it up, how do you make sure everyone gets a bit of everything?

SERVES 6

900 g (2 lb) fish trimmings
1 onion, peeled and finely chopped
2 carrots, peeled and finely chopped
2 sticks celery, peeled and finely
   chopped
1 fennel bulb, trimmed and sliced thinly
olive oil
450 g (1 lb) uncooked prawns
   (shells on)

900 g (2 lb) mussels, washed
Pernod or similar
pinch of saffron
900 g (2 lb) various white fish
175 ml (6 fl oz) double cream
2 tablespoons finely chopped chives
salt and pepper

METHOD: Cover the fish trimmings with 2 pints of water, bring to the boil and simmer gently for 30 minutes. Sauté the onion, carrots, celery and fennel in 4 tablespoons of olive oil for 15 minutes. Peel half the prawns, reserving both the flesh and the shells. Put the washed mussels in a covered pan over a moderate heat until they open. Reserve the mussels, discarding one half of each shell, and add the liquor (strained of any grit) to the vegetables along with the prawn shells and the fish stock, strained. Bring to the boil and reduce until the stock has a suitably concentrated flavour, about 10 minutes. Strain into a clean saucepan, pushing through as much of the detritus or 'body' as you can with a wooden spoon. You can complete this stage in advance, cool the liquor down and refrigerate it.

Reheat the stock and when boiling, add the Pernod and a pinch of saffron. Add the fish, starting with the firmest and finishing with the peeled and unpeeled prawns and mussels. When the last of the fish is in, wait 1 minute and turn the heat off. Stir in the cream and chives, season with salt and pepper and serve with lots of bread.

SMOKED HADDOCK AND PARSLEY MASH

Smoke a haddock and the fish takes on a faint pink hue, the whiteness of the flesh shimmering beneath the transparency of the smoke. So what is that yellow fish lying on the fishmonger's slab? It's haddock and it's smoked, but it's also dipped in dye. We are a nation that for some reason likes our smoked haddock to be vivid. For me the dye is unnecessary – orange food is something I'm happy to do without, unless, of course, its source is saffron or turmeric.

SERVES 4

900 g (2 lb) smoked haddock
850 ml (1½ pints) full-cream milk
1 bay leaf
8 peppercorns
large bunch of flat-leaf parsley
1 garlic clove
2 tablespoons finely chopped radish
1 red chilli, cored and deseeded and
  finely chopped

½ red pepper, cored, deseeded and
  finely chopped
salt and pepper
olive oil
900 g (2 lb) cooked potatoes
2 lemons, halved

METHOD: Put the haddock, cut into 8 equal-sized pieces, into a saucepan with the milk, bay leaf, peppercorns, stems from the parsley and garlic, and bring to the boil. Turn the heat right down, cover and simmer gently for 10 minutes. Carefully remove the fish and keep warm. Finely chop the parsley leaves.

Combine the radish, chilli and red pepper, season with salt and pepper and add just enough olive oil to hold the mixture together.

Strain the milk you cooked the fish in and, in a clean saucepan, heat 5 tablespoons of olive oil. As the oil heats, whisk in the potatoes along with the strained milk until you reach the desired consistency – you may require a little more or less milk. Stir the chopped parsley into the mash. Place the fish on top of the mash with some of the red pepper relish sitting on the fish. Serve with a wedge of lemon on the side.

PAN-FRIED HALIBUT WITH GREEN PEPPER SAUCE AND STEAMED GREENS

Hook a halibut and you could be in for a shock – these monsters of the sea have been known to arrive touching six feet in length. Red Indians used to fish for halibut in dugout canoes, spearing their victims and then using inflated seal skins to get them home without capsizing. Sounds a little like hard work to me – easier by far to trot up to the fishmonger, and a great deal safer.

Halibut has a tendency to dryness, so fry or grill over a high heat and then allow the fish to rest so the juices run, much as you do for steak.

SERVES 4

4 handfuls of spring greens, trimmed	*175 ml (6 fl oz) fish stock*
of any stalks	*zest and juice from 1 orange*
olive oil	*110 g (4 oz) butter, cut into cubes and*
4 halibut steaks	*chilled*
1 tablespoon dried green peppercorns	*salt and pepper*
1 glass white wine	

METHOD: Steam the greens for 3 minutes, refresh under cold water and roughly chop. Set aside. If you don't have a steamer cook in plenty of boiling salted water. Heat 3 tablespoons of olive oil and when hot, fry the halibut for 3 minutes, turn over and give it just 2 more minutes. Transfer to a low oven and allow to rest.

Pour off all the fat from the pan and add the peppercorns, wine, stock and orange zest and juice. Reduce to half its volume, lower the heat slightly and whisk in the butter, piece by piece. Return the greens to the pan and toss in the sauce. Place the greens on 4 plates, season with salt and pepper and serve the fish on top.

ROAST JOHN DORY WITH
COURGETTES AND SORREL SALSA

John Dory has a firm, robust flesh that can well handle a good roasting. It has a slight tendency to dryness, however, and so performs better when left on the bone. Trouble is, it wasn't blessed with good looks and is quite a handful with its spiky hairdo and flabby belly. Resist the temptation to fillet it, but instead ask your fishmonger to remove the head, preferably into your bag for stock making, and cut off the spikes all round the edge. He can also trim away most of the stomach lining. You should be left with a neat, usually portion-size package. If it's too big, get him to cut the fish in half, across the backbone, so you get two portions out of one fish.

SERVES 4

1 red pepper
2 tomatoes
handful of sorrel leaves, any stalky
   bits removed
salt and pepper
olive oil

4 portion-sized John Dory
plain flour
900 g (2 lb) courgettes
50 g (2 oz) butter
1 garlic clove, peeled and finely chopped
2 lemons

METHOD: Deseed and core the pepper and finely dice. Remove the seeds from the tomatoes and finely dice. Chop the sorrel roughly and mix with the pepper and tomato. Season with salt and pepper and pour in enough olive oil to bind together.

Preheat the oven to gas mark 6/400°F/200°C. Season the fish with salt and pepper, dip in plain flour and lightly brown in 3 tablespoons of olive oil. Turn over and transfer to the oven and roast for 8 minutes; remove and allow to rest.

Meanwhile trim the courgettes and cut into thin lengths. Melt the butter in a frying pan and gently sauté the courgettes for 5 minutes, tossing in the butter so they just cook through. Add the garlic, season with salt and pepper, cook for 2 more minutes and then distribute on 4 plates. Lay the John Dory on top and finish with a dollop of the sorrel salsa and a wedge of lemon.

MACKEREL TERIYAKI WITH
BEANSPROUT SALAD

I'm no fisherman, but even I have managed to hook a mackerel on the end of a fluorescent orange line thrown, without much thought, over the back of a boat. Of the two of us I'm still convinced I was the one who suffered the greatest shock. Home we went and sure enough, built a fire and cooked half a dozen mackerel, smothered slices of soda bread with thick yellow butter and washed this feast down with mugs of tea. Better than fish and chips any day.

You can buy the teriyaki sauce for this recipe in bottles, but the home-made variety has a freshness and vibrancy that is worth the extra effort. My thanks to Alastair Little, who taught me about the joys of teriyaki. Try marinating other fish, or chicken, or duck – the teriyaki adds an interesting combination of flavours which draws out and enhances the fish or meat.

SERVES 4

4 mackerel, filleted, but skin left on	*225 g (8 oz) beansprouts*
2 tablespoons soy sauce	*bunch of fresh coriander*
1 tablespoon sake (or dry white wine)	*plain flour*
1 tablespoon mirin (or sherry)	*salt and pepper*
150 g (5 oz) mangetout	*oil for frying*

METHOD: Pat the mackerel dry and place in an earthenware bowl. Combine the soy sauce, sake, mirin and 2 tablespoons of water in a saucepan and bring to the boil. Remove from the heat, pour over the mackerel and set aside for 20 minutes.

Trim the mangetout and slice as thinly as possible lengthways; mix with the beansprouts and set aside. Pick the leaves from the coriander stems and place in a bowl with some cold water – you will need about 20 leaves.

Season a tablespoon of flour with plenty of salt and pepper. Drain the fish and reserve the marinade. Pat the fish dry and roll lightly in the flour. Fry the fillets in a little oil until cooked – 1 to 2 minutes each side – remove and keep warm.

Lightly fry the beansprouts and mangetout in the remaining oil for 2 minutes. Add the marinade and toss with the vegetables. Serve the fish on top of the vegetables and sprinkle over the coriander leaves.

ROAST MONKFISH WITH
PANCETTA AND ROSEMARY

Whole monkfish look like bulldogs and are equally ugly, their puffy cheeks –
actually a great delicacy – threatening to take over the rest of their face.
Although a little troublesome to prepare – not only does the skin need to
come off, but also the stubborn membrane underneath – it has a smooth,
full-tasting milky white flesh that is wonderfully robust, making it suitable
for most types of cooking and a keen partner with even the strongest
flavours. Try buying a steak cut across the bone: it makes serving that much
easier.

SERVES 4

*900 g (2 lb) monkfish, boned and
skinned and cut into four*
salt and pepper
olive oil
*50 g (2 oz) pancetta (Italian bacon),
cut in thin slices, or unsmoked
streaky bacon*
*1 head of garlic, split into cloves, but
unpeeled*

*4 × 7.5 cm (3 inch) sprigs of
rosemary*
*450 g (1 lb) potatoes, cut into 1 cm (½
inch) slices and parboiled for 10
minutes*
bunch of chives, very finely chopped

METHOD: Preheat the oven to gas mark 6/400°F/200°C.
Season the monkfish all over with salt and pepper and coat in olive oil.
Wrap the pancetta around the fish, securing it with cocktail sticks or string.
Lay the fish on top of the garlic and rosemary in a roasting tin and roast for
15 minutes. Remove to a plate and leave in the open and switched-off oven
to rest.

Remove and discard the garlic and rosemary and add the potatoes to the
roasting tin along with 2 tablespoons of olive oil. Cook over a moderate
heat, stirring continuously, until tender and lightly brown. Put a neat pile of
the potatoes in the middle of each plate, remove the pancetta from the fish
and place the fish on top of the potatoes. Briefly grill the pancetta until
crisp, place back on top of the fish and sprinkle over the chives.

GREY MULLET WITH TOMATO PESTO

The grey mullet, no relation to the more expensive and highly regarded red mullet, is one of our most overlooked fish. Around the world it is held in higher esteem, threaded on to barbecue skewers, stuffed, or poached in coconut milk – the firm but delicate flesh is actually one of the best deals on the fishmonger's slab. I have tried every way with grey mullet and the most successful is undoubtedly roasting it whole, on the bone. This recipe, adapted from one first shown to me by Dan Evans, is wonderfully dramatic, the silver skin of the fish contrasting strongly with the yellow lemon and the red sauce.

SERVES 4

4 grey mullet	*1 tablespoon pine nuts*
salt and pepper	*2 garlic cloves*
flour	*2 dessertspoons grated Parmesan*
3 tablespoons sun-dried tomatoes in oil	*olive oil*
10 cherry tomatoes	*2 lemons*

METHOD: Preheat the oven to gas mark 7/425°F/220°C.

Season the fish with salt and pepper, making sure you press salt inside the cavity. Dust lightly in flour, dribble over a little olive oil and roast for 10–15 minutes depending on the size of the fish.

Put the sun-dried and cherry tomatoes in a food processor or liquidiser and blend for a few moments. In a dry frying pan lightly roast the pine nuts for 2 minutes until just golden. Peel, finely chop the garlic and add it along with the pine nuts and Parmesan to the tomatoes. Blend again and then pour in enough olive oil to form a paste.

Dribble the pesto on top of the roasted fish and serve with a generous wedge of lemon.

GRILLED MUSSELS WITH GARLIC, PARSLEY AND CHILLI

Mussel hunting was one of my favourite holiday activities in the west of Ireland as a child. Down on to the rocks we would go, armed with buckets to search among the wet and heavy curtains of seaweed. Home to the back-porch chatter as the barnacles were knocked off and the endless washing and scrubbing completed. It was a lot of work, but the food was free and of course there were no better mussels to be had. You can now buy farmed mussels so smooth and barnacle free they even have their beards removed, which saves a lot of time.

SERVES 4

1 × 2 kg bag mussels
2 garlic cloves, peeled and finely
  chopped
2 red chillies, deseeded and finely
  chopped

4 tomatoes, deseeded and finely chopped
2 tablespoons chopped parsley
salt and pepper
4 tablespoons breadcrumbs
olive oil

METHOD: Wash the mussels well and remove the beards as necessary. Put in a saucepan, cover with a lid and stew over a moderate heat for 5 minutes, or until the mussels open. Discard any that do not open, or any with broken shells. Break off the empty shell halves and discard, retaining the shell halves containing the mussels.

Mix together the garlic, chillies, tomatoes and parsley and season with salt and pepper. Spoon a little of this mixture into each of the mussels. Sprinkle over the breadcrumbs and dribble over a generous amount of olive oil. Place under the grill till golden and bubbling and serve with lots of bread to mop up the juices.

BAKED PLAICE WITH
STAR ANISE BEURRE BLANC

The Flemish call plaice *mooie meid*, or beautiful maiden, which apart from being more romantic, treats this sweet and delicate fish with the respect it deserves. It may be politically incorrect to encourage the comparison, but the name plaice doesn't really convey anything of the succulence and delicacy of what is, after all, perhaps our most important flat fish. I grew up on suppers of plaice fillets dipped in egg and breadcrumbs and served with wobbling spoonfuls of mayonnaise. Delicious as they are, my preference now is to bake it on the bone.

SERVES 4

5 tablespoons white wine vinegar	*4 large plaice*
8 peppercorns	*olive oil*
1 tablespoon chopped shallots	*1 glass white wine*
4–6 star anise	*salt and pepper*
225 g (8 oz) chilled butter, cubed	*2 lemons*

METHOD: Preheat the oven to gas mark 5/375°F/190°C.

Combine the vinegar with an equal quantity of water in a saucepan along with the peppercorns and shallots. Bring to the boil and reduce until you have about a tablespoon. Watch it at the end: the liquid can disappear in no time. Strain back into the saucepan and add the star anise.

Over a gentle heat, whisk in the butter, one cube at a time. The trick is to keep the heat low and emulsify the butter with the reduced liquid – if it melts too quickly it goes greasy. Keep removing the saucepan from the heat so it doesn't get too hot. When the last of the butter is added set aside, whisking every now and then.

Put the fish into a lightly oiled roasting tin, pour over the wine and season with salt and pepper. Bake for 10 minutes, or until just cooked. Serve with the beurre blanc and half a lemon per portion.

PRAWNS IN CHILLI OIL WITH
ROCKET AND TOMATO SALAD

I have a tiny freezer attached to my fridge, but at the back there is always a packet of prawns. These are uncooked and lie, wrapped in overcoats of ice, ready for that quick meal. Laid out on a plate the ice soon melts, exposing the blue-grey hue of their soft shells. I prefer to do this dish with the shells on: it encourages hands-on eating and I adore the colour. If you prefer to take the skins off beforehand, don't bin them, but roast and simmer to provide or enrich a stock. This dish will not work with cooked prawns, since the reheating dries out the flesh.

SERVES 4

450 g (1 lb) tomatoes   *salt and pepper*
4 handfuls of rocket leaves   *olive oil*
1 hot chilli, cored and deseeded   *450 g (1 lb) uncooked prawns*
1 garlic clove, peeled and finely chopped *2 lemons*

METHOD: Quarter the tomatoes and run a knife down the inside to remove the seeds, which should be discarded. Toss the tomatoes with the rocket and arrange on 4 plates. Combine the chilli, garlic and a seasoning of salt and pepper with 110 ml (4 fl oz) of olive oil.

In a frying pan heat a scant 2 tablespoons of olive oil until very hot, but not smoking. Add the prawns and toss in the heat for 2 minutes, or until the prawns are cooked. Remove with a slotted spoon and place on top of the salad. Pour over the chilli oil and serve with a wedge of lemon.

POT-ROASTED SALMON WITH
CAPERS AND BLACK OLIVES

In southern Italy in the early months of summer, you can buy fresh capers that are vivid green and inedible. Carried home they are salted and immersed in best vinegar – drawing out their sweetness – to be used in any number of wonderful dishes over the forthcoming months. Capers get something of a bashing in this country, being seen as nuggets of green sharpness with no inherent flavour. Don't blame the poor caper. Best vinegar means just that; nothing else will do. All too often the vinegar used spoils the whole effect. Search out one of the better brand names for your capers, or try the salted variety. The latter will need soaking, but have a wonderful sweet flavour to make up for the extra work.

SERVES 4

4 salmon cutlets	*175 g (6 oz) green beans*
flour	*110 g (4 oz) pitted black olives*
olive oil	*2 tablespoons capers*
salt and pepper	*175 ml (6 fl oz) fish stock*
4 carrots	*1 tablespoon chopped parsley*

METHOD: Dust the fish in flour and lightly brown in olive oil using the casserole you will use for the roasting. Season with salt and pepper and set aside. Peel and trim the carrots and cut lengthways into thin strips. Top and tail the beans and roughly chop the black olives. In the same pan lightly colour the vegetables in the hot oil for 5 minutes. Add the black olives and capers and toss in the oil.

Pour over the stock and bring to the boil, then lower the heat and lay the fish on top, covering with the lid. Cook over a moderate heat for 8 minutes, basting the fish twice during the process. Remove the fish and keep warm. Continue cooking the vegetables with the lid off until tender. Serve with the fish on top and a sprinkling of parsley.

ROAST SALMON WITH
SPICED RED CABBAGE

I had always associated red cabbage with game, casseroles and thick winter stews until a meal in Caen, in northern France, one early September. On that occasion sole was poached and served with the cabbage and the idea worked so well that I adapted it for a number of other fish recipes, including this one for salmon, which I think works the best. Eating the skin of salmon may not immediately sound like one of my more inspired suggestions, but the high heat renders it crisp and, I think, rather delicious.

SERVES 4

1 red cabbage	*pinch of cayenne pepper*
1 red onion	*110 g (4 oz) butter*
2 garlic cloves	*110 ml (4 fl oz) cassis*
olive oil	*5 tablespoons red wine vinegar*
4 star anise	*4 salmon fillets, skin attached*
2 teaspoons ground cumin	*1 glass white wine*
5 cm (2 inch) piece of ginger, grated	

METHOD: Core the cabbage and remove any damaged outer leaves. Slice finely, along with the red onion and garlic, and sauté gently in 110 ml (4 fl oz) of olive oil for 10 minutes. Stir in the spices and turn the heat up. Fry, turning continuously, for 5 minutes. Dot with the butter, pour over the cassis and vinegar, cover and simmer over a gentle heat for 30 minutes.

Turn the oven up as high as it will go. Heat a little olive oil in a frying pan that will go in the oven and put in the salmon, skin side down. Press gently down and leave to fry for 2 minutes. Turn over, transfer to the oven and roast for 6 minutes. Remove and allow to rest for 5 minutes. Pour off any excess fat and deglaze the pan over a moderate heat with the white wine. Serve the fish on top of the cabbage with the roasting juices.

SAUTÉED SARDINE FILLET WITH
PARSLEY PESTO AND CUCUMBER SPAGHETTI

Grilled sardines, along with tomato salads, are for me one of the summer's perfect starters. It's a hot evening; the children are tucked up in bed; you are drinking chilled, fresh white wine outside as the sardines grill over the barbecue, and your main course is but an arm's stretch away. My only grumble is with the enormous amount of detritus left on my plate at the end. For sweet and delicious as sardines are, the proportion of edible meat to head, bones and skin seems extremely small. This is a somewhat neater way of serving sardines – the filleting is easy and really does take very little time. This recipe works best with largish sardines, or even small herrings.

SERVES 4

900 g (2 lb) sardines
salt and pepper
5 tablespoons breadcrumbs
3 dessertspoons grated Parmesan
small saucer of milk
flour
2 eggs, lightly whisked

olive oil
1 garlic clove, peeled and finely chopped
2 dessertspoons pine nuts
large bunch of parsley
lemon juice
1 cucumber

METHOD: Lay each sardine on a chopping board. Insert a sharp knife behind the head of the fish, cut down to the backbone and then work the blade towards the tail using the backbone as a guide. Turn the fish over and repeat. Cut the thin flesh off the bottom of the belly.

Wash each of the fillets carefully, pat dry and season with salt and pepper. Combine the breadcrumbs and Parmesan in a shallow bowl. Dip each of the fillets in the milk, then in the flour and then in the egg. Roll them in the breadcrumbs and Parmesan, gently pressing so each fillet picks up as much of the mixture as possible.

Put 110 ml (4 fl oz) of olive oil into a liquidiser along with the garlic, pine nuts, parsley and a seasoning of salt and pepper. Blitz for 15 seconds and then add lemon juice to taste. Using a mandolin, cut the cucumber into spaghetti-like strands and arrange on 4 plates.

Heat 5 tablespoons of olive oil in a frying pan and gently sauté the fillets until crisp and golden. Drain on kitchen paper and serve on top of the cucumber with a generous dollop of the pesto.

SCALLOPS WITH CRISPY BACON AND MINTED SPLIT-PEA PURÉE

Scallops are an introspective bunch. They have about 50 eyes round the rim of their shells, and as they propel themselves forward, scalloping along the sea bed, the eyes check for danger behind, totally ignoring the possibility of head-on collisions. Scallops are often cleaned at sea, so the shells never reach the fishmonger. This is a shame, since most of the rest of the meat is edible, suitable for fish stock or soups.

If you can get them in their shells they are easy to open. Hold the deep shell in the palm of your hand and slip a knife into the rear, right-hand corner. This releases the adductor muscle holding the shell closed. Scoop it out: this is the bit you are going to eat, along with the coral. Discard the eyes and gills, the black bit attached to the coral and the hard gristly bit attached to the disc. The rest will do well in tomorrow's fish soup.

SERVES 4

4 rashers streaky bacon	*bunch of mint, finely chopped*
olive oil	*5 tablespoons single cream*
110 g (4 oz) split green peas, rinsed in	*salt and pepper*
several changes of water	*16 scallops (12 if they are large)*
1 onion, peeled and finely chopped	*2 lemons*

METHOD: Fry the bacon in a little olive oil until crisp, remove, drain on kitchen paper, roughly chop and reserve. In the same pan add the peas, onion and 570 ml (1 pint) of water. Bring to the boil, cover and simmer until the peas are tender, about 15–20 minutes. Allow to cool, liquidise and push through a sieve. Reheat, stir in the mint, cream and salt and pepper to taste. Add a little water if it looks too thick.

Fry the scallops on both sides until lightly golden, remove and season well with salt and pepper. Add the pea purée to the frying pan, scrape up the juices and transfer to four plates. Arrange the scallops on top of the purée, scatter over the bacon, add a wedge of lemon and serve.

POACHED SEA TROUT WITH BEURRE BLANC, GREEN BEANS AND NEW POTATOES

The sea or salmon trout has successfully skimmed off the best characteristics of both the salmon and the trout, most notably dumping the salmon's tendency to dry up. Its beautiful pink colour is one of its most charming qualities – that and the closely knit texture of the skin, which is so similar to that of the trout. The best of both worlds, and a little more, this sweet, delicate fish really is one of the joys of an English summer. Beurre blanc is a fairly simple sauce to make and one of the classic accompaniments.

If you need an excuse to buy a fish kettle, then this is it. Buy a big one: there is nothing more frustrating than trying to stuff a fish into a kettle too small. Sea trout deserve the best treatment.

SERVES 4

450 g (1 lb) new potatoes, wiped clean *8 peppercorns*
salt and pepper *1 blade of mace*
450 g (1 lb) green beans, trimmed *1.125 kg (2½ lb) sea trout, cleaned*
white wine vinegar *225 g (8 oz) best unsalted butter, cut*
1 tablespoon shallots, finely chopped *into cubes and chilled*

METHOD: Cook the potatoes in boiling salted water until almost, but not quite done. Remove and refresh under cold water. Do the same with the beans. Leave the pan of water at the back of the stove, covered, over a gentle heat.

Put 5 tablespoons of vinegar and the same quantity of water in a small saucepan with the shallots, peppercorns and mace and reduce until you have about 1 tablespoon. Strain into a bowl.

Bring sufficient water to cover the fish to the boil in the fish kettle. Generously salt and then lower the fish in. Bring back to a gentle, rolling boil and simmer for 10–15 minutes. To test, pull the fish up on the tray and try to remove a little of the back fin. When cooked, this should come out with a gentle but firm tug. If it doesn't, lower the tray back in for 5 minutes and test again. Leave the fish on the tray above the water to rest.

Place the bowl containing the reduced vinegar over a pan of gently simmering water and whisk in the butter cubes, one at a time so it emulsifies with the vinegar. Season with salt and pepper and set aside, near, but not on the heat.

Return the vegetables to the boiling water for 1 minute to heat through and distribute on 4 plates. Divide up the sea trout and place on top of the vegetables. Put a generous spoonful of the sauce on the side, serving the rest in a warmed bowl.

GRILLED TUNA FISH WITH
SOY DRESSING AND
PICKLED GINGER

Up until the end of the last century entire communities along the east coast of Spain and the west coast of Italy down as far as Sicily would turn out for the tuna fishing. These sleek, often enormous fish would be chased into an interconnecting series of anchored nets, eventually to be drawn up to the surface where the fish would be killed with harpoon-like spears. Processing them took a long time, but every single part of the fish was used, right down to the fins, which would be ground up and used as fertiliser. The Japanese go wild about tuna fish and I can quite see their point: it is moist, with a good firm texture and that sweet, salty tang that is so much the essence of fresh fish.

SERVES 4

10 cm (4 inch) cube of ginger, peeled	*5 tablespoons soy sauce*
and cut into matchstick strips	*4 star anise*
200 ml (7 fl oz) rice vinegar	*2 garlic cloves*
5 tablespoons dry sherry	*4 tuna steaks*

METHOD: Blanch the ginger in boiling water for 10 seconds, drain and refresh under cold water. Put in a bowl with all but 2 tablespoons of the vinegar and set aside. Combine the remaining vinegar with the sherry, soy sauce, star anise and garlic in a saucepan. Add 110 ml (4 fl oz) of water and reduce over a gentle heat until about half the original volume.

Grill the tuna fish for 2 minutes either side and allow to rest in a low oven for 2 minutes. Serve with the ginger on top and a few spoonfuls of the soy dressing, strained.

Poultry & Game

Chicken is one of the most versatile foods available. Simply roasted, or cooked with spices or herbs, it works alone and in partnership equally well. Add to chicken, other poultry like quail, poussin and guinea fowl – which are all widely available – and there is a whole family to work with. And that is before you even start on the game.

There is a world of difference between the glories of French Bresse and the grim depths of mechanically fed caged birds – known as broilers – whose existence is merely part of some large machine. Concentrate on the free-range birds, whose flavour is infinitely superior and for only a few pence more. As with eggs, however, free-range is a term open to abuse, so make sure you use a reputable supplier. When you think of how fantastic a roast chicken can be – moist, full of flavour, golden and crispy with a depth and range of tastes – you realise it can't really be that cheap if it is going to be good.

Game is something of a national institution, but only recently has it become widely available in supermarkets. Feast throughout the autumn and winter on grouse, partridge, pigeons, mallard, hare, woodcock – all of which offer fantastic eating. Try grouse and game chips for the traditional approach, or pheasant steamed with ginger and Chinese cabbage for a more modern version.

Game comes in various states of highness, determined both by its age and in many cases by the length of time it is hung. For well-hung game you need a traditional game dealer, who in many cases will hang to order. Supermarket game tends not to be hung for long, giving a milder, less developed taste. Trial and error is the only way to decide on your preferences.

BREAST OF CHICKEN STUFFED WITH AUBERGINE PURÉE

Aubergines seem to have an ability to keep other food moist. This is a particular asset when they are partnered with chicken breasts, which are so lean that they have a tendency to dry out. I first did this recipe when I had a roasted aubergine left over, but I now often roast a few extra on purpose. If you are starting from scratch, prick the aubergine several times and roast in a moderate oven until soft, about 20-30 minutes.

SERVES 4

4 large outside Savoy cabbage leaves
1 small onion, peeled and finely
 chopped
olive oil
1 garlic clove, peeled and finely chopped
1 teaspoon ground cumin

1 roasted aubergine, flesh removed and
 skin discarded
bunch of thyme
salt and pepper
4 chicken breasts

METHOD: Preheat the oven to gas mark 6/400°F/200°C.

Blanch the cabbage leaves in boiling water for 2 minutes, drain, refresh under cold water and set aside. Soften the onion in 2 tablespoons of olive oil for 10 minutes, add the garlic and cumin and 2 minutes later the aubergine. Remove from the heat and add a teaspoon of chopped thyme and a seasoning of salt and pepper. Mix well.

Slice the chicken breasts in two, leaving them attached by one edge. Brush lightly with olive oil and place a tablespoon of the stuffing in the middle of each one. Fold over the flesh and then wrap with the cabbage leaves. Tie each breast up with string and roast in the oven for 15–20 minutes. Allow to rest for 5 minutes before slicing and serving with any of the aubergine mixture remaining. I leave the cabbage leaves on, but you may wish to remove them.

BRAISED CHICKEN WITH CHORIZO, CHICKPEAS AND TOASTED ALMONDS

In Barcelona many of the shops selling chickpeas and other pulses also sell bowls of them already cooked, the long process of soaking and boiling completed by the owner of the shop. Women queue – why is it always women? – for the contents of their stew, to be eaten when all the family return in the middle of the day for lunch. This custom of going home for lunch is fast disappearing even in Barcelona, an indulgence in today's world. We may lack similar shops, but tinned chickpeas are widely available and the closest we can get to avoiding all the hard work. The nutty succulence of chickpeas makes them one of my favourite pulses.

SERVES 4

1 whole chicken, jointed into 10 pieces
4 chorizo (Spanish sausages available from delicatessens and most supermarkets)
2 red onions, peeled and chopped
olive oil

salt and pepper
1 × 400 g (14 oz) tin of chickpeas
1 glass white wine
pinch of saffron
bunch of parsley, finely chopped
50 g (2 oz) flaked almonds

METHOD: In a casserole large enough to hold everything, lightly colour the chicken, chorizo and red onion in 5 tablespoons of oil. Season with salt and pepper, lower the heat and braise for 20 minutes, covered, turning frequently to prevent anything sticking.

Rinse the chickpeas under cold water and add to the chicken, along with the wine, saffron, parsley and a seasoning of salt and pepper. Continue to cook over a low heat for 10 minutes. Lightly toast the almonds in a dry frying pan until just coloured. Serve the chicken and chorizo with the almonds sprinkled on top.

BRAISED CHICKEN WITH
CELERIAC AND GARLIC MASH

Chicken pieces are a great help to the busy cook, eliminating the need to carve, or to decide who gets which piece of the bird, the source of more family arguments than I care to remember. Jointing a chicken is not difficult: a sharp knife and a little patience will have the bird in pieces within minutes. I mention this because some of the better quality birds do not come in portions, but whole, and as is so often the case, the better the bird, the better the dish.

SERVES 4

8 chicken pieces with skin attached
olive oil
salt and pepper
1 small celeriac, peeled and cut into
  2.5 cm (1 inch) cubes
1 head of garlic, split into cloves, but
  unpeeled

175 ml (6 fl oz) milk
900 g (2 lb) cooked potatoes, peeled
  and mashed (these can be cold)
bunch of chives, finely chopped

METHOD: Preheat the oven to gas mark 6/400°F/200°C.

Toss the chicken pieces in olive oil, season with salt and pepper and place in a roasting tin. Blanch the celeriac in boiling salted water for 2 minutes, drain, refresh under cold water and pat dry. Add the celeriac and garlic to the roasting tin and toss so they are also coated with olive oil (you may need a little more oil). Put in the preheated oven and cook for 25 minutes. If you are using breast meat, this should be added 10 minutes after the other pieces. Remove the chicken pieces and celeriac and keep warm.

Roughly mash the roasted garlic cloves and place in a small saucepan together with the milk. Pour in 5 tablespoons of olive oil and heat until it almost reaches boiling point. Strain and whisk into the cooked potato over a moderate heat until you reach the desired consistency and the potato is hot. Season with salt and pepper. Serve the chicken and celeriac on top of the mash with a sprinkling of chives.

BRAISED CHICKEN WITH
SOFT POLENTA

Polenta is often served grilled or fried in slices, but it usually starts life as a soft purée similar in consistency to mash. This mound of wobbling maize, golden yellow in colour and with a sweet smell, is the sort of comfort food I crave on dark nights. You can buy so-called instant polenta but for my money it's not a patch on the real thing. Anyway, part of the joy of polenta is to have it simmering, volcano-like, on the back of the cooker, its plopping yellow molten surface interrupted by the odd stir of a wooden spoon. If you use an instant version, follow the directions on the packet.

SERVES 4

salt and pepper
275 g (10 oz) polenta
4 small red onions, peeled and
  quartered
4 chicken legs, with thighs attached
olive oil

225 g (½ lb) largish mushrooms
1 garlic clove, peeled and finely chopped
1 glass white wine
175 ml (6 fl oz) chicken stock
bunch of thyme, chopped
bunch of parsley, finely chopped

METHOD: Bring 3 pints of salted water to the boil in a covered pan, remove the lid and pour in the polenta in a steady stream, stirring all the time. Set over a low heat at the back of the stove and cook, uncovered, for 40 minutes, stirring every now and then to prevent sticking. You will end up with a crust of polenta when you empty the pan, but this can be soaked off in hot water.

Lightly colour the red onions and chicken legs in 2 tablespoons of olive oil for 5 minutes in a casserole. Remove the chicken and add the mushrooms. You may need a little more oil but take care – the mushrooms will yield it up later. Sauté for 5 minutes, then return the chicken and add the garlic. Cover and braise over a low heat for 10 minutes. Add the white wine and stock and continue to cook for 15 minutes, or until the chicken is cooked. Remove from the heat, uncover and allow to rest for 10 minutes before sprinkling over the thyme. Check seasoning and serve with the polenta and a generous sprinkling of parsley.

CHICKEN 'SATAY' WITH PICKLED CHILLIES AND VEGETABLE NOODLES

Pickling is traditionally seen as a way of preserving food and is often thought to take hours, require endless pans and preserving jars, and demand the hygienic conditions of an operating theatre lest some foreign body creep, unannounced, into the proceedings. While hygiene is obviously important, some of the best pickles take only a few moments and will certainly keep well in the fridge for a few weeks, even if they are but briefly immersed in vinegar. Anyway, who wants to spend months eating jars of the same pickle? It's much more fun to pickle small amounts of different flavours. The satay sauce is adapted from a recipe of Shri Owen's, who rightly points up the dangers of using peanut butter as a short cut. The resulting paste has a dull, lifeless quality about it which rather spoils the point.

SERVES 4

large handful of chillies
275 ml (½ pint) white wine vinegar
50 g (2 oz) caster sugar
5 tablespoons vegetable oil
110 g (4 oz) unsalted, skinned raw
  peanuts
1 garlic clove, peeled and finely chopped
1 tablespoon finely chopped shallots
salt and pepper
pinch of cayenne pepper
1 tablespoon soy sauce

juice of 1 lemon
4 handfuls of broad Chinese noodles
bunch of radishes, cleaned and roughly
  chopped
1 cucumber, peeled, deseeded and cut
  into julienne strips
110 g (4 oz) beansprouts, washed
bunch of spring onions, trimmed and
  finely sliced
450 g (1 lb) cooked chicken, shredded
bunch of coriander

METHOD: Blanch the chillies in boiling water for 1 minute, drain, refresh and pat dry. Bring the vinegar and caster sugar to the boil, pour over the chillies and set aside.

Heat the vegetable oil and fry the peanuts for 5 minutes. Remove the peanuts with a slotted spoon and drain on kitchen paper. Drain off all but 1 tablespoon of the oil and discard. In a liquidiser or food processor blitz the garlic, shallots, a seasoning of salt and pepper, the cayenne pepper and soy sauce with 275 ml (½ pint) of water. Add this to the hot oil and fry for 2 minutes. Blend the peanuts in the liquidiser or food processor – no need to wash it out – into a paste and add this to the garlic and shallot mixture. Bring to the boil and simmer gently for 10 minutes. Remove, add the lemon juice, pour into a bowl and allow to cool.

Cook the noodles according to the instructions and toss with the vegetables and 2 tablespoons of vegetable oil. Mix the chicken with the satay sauce and distribute on top. Arrange a few chillies on each plate and serve with a generous quantity of coriander leaves.

If you blanch more chillies, you can add them to the same vinegar. They will keep for a few weeks in the fridge, provided the liquid covers the chillies.

ROAST CHICKEN THIGHS WITH
SALSA VERDE AND BROCCOLI

This recipe is about as instant as I like my food to be. A packet of chicken thighs, some fresh herbs and a bunch of broccoli bought on the way home, a bit of chopping when I get there and that's it: a feast of tender meat and lots of finger licking. This sauce will keep in the fridge covered with olive oil for a few days and goes well with almost any grilled meat or fish. It also goes rather well when spread on crusty bread, a dangerous move for the cook who, in my case, can then remain rooted to the spot, bread in one hand, knife in the other and not much action on the cooking front.

SERVES 4

12 chicken thighs
olive oil
salt and pepper
2 lemons
2 garlic cloves, peeled and finely
  chopped

bunch of parsley
bunch of coriander
1 teaspoon Dijon mustard
2 tablespoons capers, drained and
  rinsed
450 g (1 lb) broccoli, trimmed

METHOD: Preheat the oven to gas mark 6/400°F/200°C.

Put the chicken thighs in a bowl along with 5 tablespoons of olive oil, a generous seasoning of salt and pepper, the juice from 1 of the lemons and 1 of the garlic cloves. Toss so the thighs are well coated, transfer to a roasting tin and put in the oven for 20 minutes, or until tender. Allow to rest for 5 minutes.

To make the salsa, put the remaining garlic in a liquidiser or food processor, along with the parsley and coriander leaves, mustard and capers. Blitz until roughly chopped and then dribble in enough olive oil to form a thick consistency. Remove to a bowl and add lemon juice to taste.

Steam or boil the broccoli until cooked and serve with the chicken thighs on top and the salsa dribbled over.

HOME-SMOKED CHICKEN WITH AVOCADO, MUSTARD AND TOMATO SALSA

Smoking was traditionally used as a means of preserving food, the smoke killing off unwanted bacteria and generally drying out the food so it could be kept for a period when things were scarce. As with many other methods of preservation, the taste and texture of the food was altered without altogether changing the character of whatever was being soaked. Thankfully we are now able to use fridges for storing food and can therefore concentrate on the flavours rather than on the need to preserve. This recipe gives the humble and useful chicken breast a rather interesting flavour.

SERVES 4

450 g (1 lb) ripe tomatoes	*white wine vinegar*
2 ripe avocados	*salt and pepper*
1 red pepper	*1 cup of tea*
1 heaped teaspoon black mustard seeds	*1 tablespoon sugar*
1 dessertspoon Dijon mustard	*1 heaped tablespoon of rice*
olive oil	*4 chicken breasts*

METHOD: Cut the tomatoes into quarters and slide a knife inside to remove the seeds. Chop the tomatoes into fine dice and put in a bowl. Peel, destone and similarly chop the avocados. Core, deseed and finely chop the red pepper and add both, along with the mustard seeds and Dijon mustard, to the tomatoes. Pour in 75 ml (3 fl oz) of olive oil, 2 teaspoons of vinegar, a seasoning of salt and pepper and gently stir everything together.

Line a wok with tin foil and pour in the tea, sugar and rice. Place the chicken pieces on a wire rack about 5 cm (2 inches) above the tea mixture. Put a lid or piece of tin foil over the whole assembly and place over a moderate heat for 15–20 minutes. If you can, remove the lid outside, as there tends to be a bit of smoke. Serve the chicken on top of the salsa.

To remove the stone from the avocado: hold the avocado half in one hand with a tea towel and bring a large carving knife down smartly on the stone, twist and remove.

ROAST CHICKEN AND BREAD SAUCE

No wonder so much time and effort has been put into trying to get roast chicken on to the nation's dining tables: it can be one of the most delicious feasts, full of flavour and contrasting textures. The trouble is, all too often the effort is for nothing; with chicken, as with so many edible birds, breed and lifestyle mean all. Buy carefully.

Good ingredients are just as important for bread sauce, one of those dishes that hovers between sublime success and boring disappointment. Lumps and lack of flavour have tainted its reputation unduly, but this Christmas sauce should be extended to the rest of the winter. A full-textured bread is essential – no sliced white here. It also needs to be finished at the last minute and seasoned well.

SERVES 4

1 chicken	*3 cloves*
4 sprigs of tarragon	*nutmeg*
2 garlic cloves, unpeeled	*275 ml (½ pint) full-cream milk*
1 lemon, quartered	*50 g (2 oz) fresh breadcrumbs*
50 g (2 oz) butter	*cayenne pepper*
salt and pepper	*2 tablespoons double cream*
1 onion	

METHOD: Preheat the oven to gas mark 6/400°F/200°C.

Stuff the chicken cavity with the tarragon, garlic and lemon. Rub the butter all over the bird, paying particular attention to the breast, and season with salt and pepper. Roast the bird on its side for 20 minutes, turn on its other side for 20 minutes and finally turn breast-side up for a further 20–25 minutes, or until the bird is cooked. Allow to rest for 10 minutes.

Stud the onion with the cloves and place in a saucepan together with a grating of nutmeg and the milk. Gently bring to the boil, pull off the heat and set aside to infuse. This step can be done in advance. Remove the onion and cloves, bring to the boil and whisk in the breadcrumbs. Season with salt and pepper and a pinch of cayenne pepper. Cook over the lowest heat for 2 minutes, remove from the heat and whisk in the cream. Serve with the chicken and any juices in the pan.

BRAISED DUCK WITH
PAK CHOI AND OYSTER SAUCE

I used to be much more inclined to roast duck at a high heat, but the benefits of slowly braising it so the fat is rendered down are on balance, I think, more appealing (although I am not quite convinced I want to say a permanent goodbye to crisply roasted duck, which features in the next recipe). This method also has the added advantage of not filling your kitchen with clouds of fat-induced duck smoke.

Pak choi, also known as bok choi, mustard greens and Chinese white cabbage, is a bit like Swiss chard, or spinach, and can be treated in much the same way. Try blanching it, for example, and then bake with bechamel sauce and Parmesan.

SERVES 4

2 large duck breasts
110 ml (4 fl oz) soy sauce
5 tablespoons dry sherry
2.5 cm (1 inch) piece of ginger, peeled
1 garlic clove
pinch of cayenne pepper

450 g (1 lb) pak choi, picked over and
   stems trimmed (available from
   Chinese supermarkets and some of
   the larger supermarkets)
oyster sauce

METHOD: Prick the fat sides of the duck breasts with a carving fork, place in the sink and pour over a kettle of boiling water. Pat dry and set aside. Combine the soy sauce, sherry, ginger, garlic and cayenne in a saucepan with 150 ml (5 fl oz) of water. Bring to the boil and simmer for 10 minutes, uncovered.

Cut the duck breasts into 2.5 cm (1 inch) pieces and add to the soy mixture. Cover, lower the heat and cook slowly for 30 minutes, or until the meat is tender, stirring every so often. Cut the pak choi lengthways into quarters and stir into the duck. Cook for a further 5 minutes. Remove from the heat, stir in 2 tablespoons of the oyster sauce and serve.

CRISPY DUCK SALAD WITH
PICKLED GINGER AND WALNUTS

Pickles are supposed to be making something of a comeback after years of isolation. In the past, preservation meant strong vinegar and caution on the part of the pickler, which often resulted in the flavours of the original ingredient disappearing in clouds of acid. Gentle pickling subtly alters the flavour of the ingredients, somehow changing them while inherently leaving them the same. Ginger is one of the most accommodating spices, working well with sweet and savoury dishes and having enough power to cut the fattiness of this dish. You can pickle your own – see box below – but the Chinese and Japanese commercial versions I've tried are extremely good.

SERVES 4

1 Aylesbury duck, jointed into 4 (2 breasts and 2 legs and thighs)
salt and pepper
3 thin slices of garlic
olive oil

2 teaspoons balsamic vinegar
4 generous handfuls of salad leaves
oil for frying
4 dessertspoons walnut kernels
4 dessertspoons pickled ginger

METHOD: Arrange the duck pieces on a piece of tin foil in the top of your steamer. Season generously with salt and pepper and steam for 30 minutes, or until the duck is tender. (You can steam the duck pieces and then finish the dish later.)

Mash the garlic with a seasoning of salt and pepper in a salad bowl until you get a pulp. Any bits of garlic are to be avoided; it really does need to be a pulp. Whisk in 5 tablespoons of olive oil, followed by the balsamic vinegar. Toss the salad leaves in the dressing and arrange on 4 plates.

Heat a little oil in a frying pan and sauté the duck pieces, skin-side down, until it crisps up. Turn over, cook for a further minute and place on the salad leaves. Sprinkle over the walnuts and ginger and serve.

Pickled ginger: Peel and thinly slice 110 g (4 oz) of ginger. Mix with enough lemon juice to cover and 2 dessertspoons caster sugar. Cover and store in the fridge. You can use it after about 4 days.

DUCK BREASTS WITH
SICHUAN PEPPERCORNS AND
CRISP VEGETABLE SALAD

My irregular trips to Chinese supermarkets continue to be a source of discovery. Endless packets curiously labelled, unrecognisable cuts of meat, strange and wonderful vegetables and fruit – all accompanied by the hustle and bustle of trading in an exotic and, for me at any rate, completely unrecognisable language. One of my best discoveries on one of these hectic shopping trips was Sichuan peppercorns. These are the red-brown berries of a plant native to Sichuan and western China. They lack the burning hotness of black peppercorns, and have an oddly contradictory cooling quality and delicious smell – all a perfect foil to the richness of duck.

SERVES 4

1 tablespoon sesame seeds	*110 g (4 oz) beansprouts*
4 Aylesbury duck breasts	*50 g (2 oz) water chestnuts*
2 tablespoons Sichuan peppercorns	*2.5 cm (1 inch) piece of ginger, grated*
110 g (4 oz) bamboo shoots	*sesame oil*
225 g (½ lb) mangetout	*soy sauce*

METHOD: In a dry frying pan briefly fry the sesame seeds until they colour, about 30 seconds. Remove and allow to cool. Prick the fat of the duck breasts with a fork, place in the sink and pour over a kettle of boiling water. Roughly crush the peppercorns in a pestle and mortar. Preheat the oven to gas mark 4/350°F/180°C. Reheat the dry frying pan until quite hot and place the duck breasts, fat-side down, in the pan. Sauté over a moderate heat until the skin begins to brown and the fat starts to run. Turn the breasts over and with a wooden spoon press the peppercorns into the fat. Transfer the pan to the oven and roast for 15 minutes. Allow the duck to rest for at least 5 minutes, better if it is 10.

Blanch the bamboo shoots in boiling water for 1 minute, drain and refresh under cold water. Chop, along with the mangetout, into slivers and combine with the beansprouts and water chestnuts. Toss with the sesame seeds, grated ginger, 2 tablespoons of sesame oil and a dash of soy sauce to taste.

Serve the duck breast, neatly sliced, on top of the vegetable salad.

DUCK CONFIT WITH
BRAISED RED CABBAGE

There is no doubt the preparation and cooking of this dish is unlikely to be something you will do at the end of a hard day, but I have included it because once prepared, duck confit is almost instant food. No wonder it is served so widely in French restaurants. Flashed under a grill, or cooked in a hot oven, it is ready in minutes, to be served with mash, or something like the braised cabbage (which can be reheated) in this recipe. Each autumn I now prepare about 10 duck legs like this, and they sit in the cool corner of my kitchen in a French crock bought specifically for that purpose. When I get home late, I prise a few out of their fat and flash under the grill – 15 minutes is my record time from grill to table so far. Some butchers sell the goose fat; otherwise try good delicatessens, food halls or some of the meat mail-order companies. If you have any left over, it makes the best roast and sautéed potatoes, or you can start again with more duck legs. Longevity depends on cleanliness: everything must be spotless.

SERVES 10

2–3 tablespoons coarse sea salt (fine
    salt will not do)
4 garlic cloves, peeled and finely
    chopped
bunch of thyme
10 duck legs (order them in advance
    from your butcher)
2.25 kg (5 lb) tinned goose fat
1 large red cabbage

olive oil
2 onions, peeled and cut into
    half-moon slices
4 star anise
7.5 cm (3 inch) stick of cinnamon
1 head of garlic, unpeeled
½ glass cassis
salt and pepper

METHOD: Combine the coarse sea salt, garlic and thyme and press gently into the exposed flesh of the duck. Place, skin-side down, in an earthenware dish and cover with cling film. Leave in the fridge for 2 days, turning the legs over after the first day. Rinse the legs under cold water and pat dry.

Gently heat the goose fat over a moderate flame in a casserole large enough to accommodate the duck legs – take care, the fat becomes extremely hot. Slide the duck into the fat and simmer over the gentlest heat for 1 hour, or until the duck is tender. Remove with a slotted spoon to a clean earthenware storage container. Spoon over enough fat to cover, leaving any juices from the meat behind (these are delicious, but reduce the keeping qualities of the confit). The duck can stay like this for about 2 months in the fridge. To reheat, melt the fat from around the duck and grill or roast until hot and crispy.

For the cabbage, remove the outer leaves, core and cut into thin slices. Heat 3 tablespoons of olive oil in a saucepan and, when hot, add the cabbage and onions, tossing them so everything is coated in the oil. Turn the heat down, put on the lid and let the cabbage and onion cook for 5 minutes. Add the star anise, cinnamon stick, garlic and cassis, and season with salt and pepper. Cover and cook over the lowest possible heat for 1 hour, turning every so often to make sure nothing sticks.

BRAISED DUCK WITH GREEN PEPPER AND BLACK BEAN SAUCE

I usually leave green peppers on the shelf, disliking their sour flavour, but they are perfect for this dish, cutting through the duck and behaving as the ideal partner to the fermented black beans. These have a wonderful earthy taste and a saltiness that is curiously powerful and subtle at the same time.

SERVES 4

2 small ducks, jointed
2 green peppers, cored, deseeded and
   cut into 2.5 cm (1 inch) pieces
2 red onions, peeled and quartered
1 garlic clove, peeled and finely chopped
2.5 cm (1 inch) piece of ginger, peeled
   and finely chopped
1 teaspoon each of cumin, coriander,
   star anise

generous pinch of cinnamon
570 ml (1 pint) chicken stock
2 dessertspoons fermented black beans
   (available in most ethnic stores,
   usually in tins)
salt and pepper

METHOD: Colour the duck pieces – by placing them fat-side down in the pan, the duck fat should start to run as soon as the heat raises the temperature – for 5 minutes and remove. If there is too much fat, pour a little off, then sauté the peppers and onion for 5 minutes. Add the garlic, ginger and spices and continue frying for 2 minutes. Return the duck, pour over the stock, and add the black beans. Season (remember the beans are salty) and cover. Simmer for 40 minutes over a gentle heat, or until the duck is cooked.

Remove the duck and keep warm while reducing the sauce by half. Serve with rice or plain potatoes.

ROAST MALLARD WITH
THYME AND GARLIC MASH

The mallard is a dabbler, mucking about in shallow water feeding on vegetation and sticking its head underwater in the hope of finding some juicy morsel. Not all wild ducks follow the same pattern, however – some take the underwater bit very seriously and have a habit of ditching their veg in preference for fish, which rather flavours their meat. Luckily the other wild ducks most commonly found – teal and widgeon – are also dabblers, so you shouldn't have too much to worry about.

SERVES 4

2 mallard	*4 garlic cloves, unpeeled*
4 bay leaves	*275 ml (10 fl oz) milk*
salt and pepper	*5 tablespoons olive oil*
175 ml (6 fl oz) white wine	*900 g (2 lb) cooked potato, mashed*
bunch of thyme	

METHOD: Preheat the oven to gas mark 6/400°F/200°C.

Prick the ducks all over with a carving fork, put them in the sink, pour over a kettle of boiling water and pat dry. Stuff the bay leaves inside the ducks, season well with salt and pepper, place in a roasting pan and roast for 25 minutes. Turn the oven off, transfer the ducks to a plate, return to the oven and leave the door ajar to allow the ducks to rest for 10 minutes.

Drain the fat from the pan, place over a moderate heat and deglaze the pan with the white wine. Allow to reduce to about 110 ml (4 fl oz) and keep warm. Reserve a few of the thyme leaves for decoration and put the remainder of the bunch, a scant handful, along with the garlic, milk and olive oil, into a saucepan. Slowly bring to the boil over a low heat so the flavours infuse. Strain through a sieve and whisk into the potatoes over a moderate heat so they are heated through – you may need more milk. Season with salt and pepper.

To serve the duck, cut the legs off and remove the breast from the bone of the duck by easing a sharp knife along the breastbone. Place on a chopping board and slice diagonally across. Serve on top of the mash with a little of the reduced sauce at the side and sprinkle over the reserved thyme leaves.

WILD DUCK BRAISED WITH CABBAGE AND PORCINI

Mallard, just one of several species of wild duck, is, like myself, keen on eating. So enthusiastic is this creature that, if allowed, it will quaff vast quantities of food which quickly becomes fat – a quality unwanted in this already oily bird. In the wild this is rarely a problem as they generally work quite hard to stay alive. But be careful about who you buy from. Mallard are increasingly being farmed, much like pheasants, and the result is not always a pleasure to eat; flabby and tasteless, they quickly lose their gamy quality which seems largely to miss the point.

SERVES 4

2 mallard, the skin pricked over with a sharp fork	*10 g (½ oz) dried porcini, soaked in warm water for 20 minutes*
1 onion, peeled and finely chopped	*110 ml (4 fl oz) brandy*
2 garlic cloves, peeled and finely chopped	*1 glass white wine*
	salt and pepper
1 Savoy cabbage	*110 g (4 oz) butter*

METHOD: Preheat the oven to gas mark 4/350°F/180°C.

In a casserole large enough to hold all the ingredients, lightly brown the mallard. You are unlikely to need any oil for this if you start with the breasts, which will release some of the fat from under the skin. Set aside. Sauté the onion in the fat for 10 minutes without colouring, add the garlic and continue cooking for 2 minutes.

Remove the outer leaves from the cabbage as well as the core, finely shred and put in the casserole with the onion, tossing so it is well coated in the fat. Drain the porcini, add to the onion mixture, mix well and replace the duck, nestling them in among the cabbage so they are on their sides. Pour over the brandy and set alight. When the flames have died down, add the white wine, season with salt and pepper and place half the butter on top of each bird. Cover with tin foil and a lid and put in the oven for 40 minutes, turning the birds over after 20 minutes. You will need to baste 2 or 3 times during the cooking.

Remove the birds and allow to rest for 10 minutes. Cut off the legs and then the breast by sliding a carving knife along the breastbone. Each breast should come away easily and then can be cut into thick slices on a chopping board. Serve the breasts and legs on top of the cabbage and porcini with the juice spooned over the top.

GAME STEW WITH CHESTNUTS

Chestnuts are one of those rare, and consequently exciting foods, that still cling stubbornly to the idea of seasonality. You can buy them tinned, jarred and vac-packed, but there is nothing to beat the ritual of skinning fresh chestnuts – burned fingertips, the odd dodgy one and that warm winter smell.

Marinating meat tenderises it, alters the flavour and reduces the cooking time. Overnight marinating means this thick winter stew will be cooked in an hour, just enough time to open a few bottles of claret. You can now buy packs of assorted game in most of the supermarkets, although I would still urge a visit to your butcher or game dealer.

SERVES 6

450 g (1 lb) venison, cubed
1 hare, jointed into 8, ribcage and
front end removed
275 ml (½ pint) red wine
4 carrots, peeled and cut into 5 cm (2
inch) wedges
4 sticks celery, trimmed and cut into 5
cm (2 inch) lengths
2 red onions, peeled and quartered
2 garlic cloves, peeled and finely
chopped

2 bay leaves
110 ml (4 fl oz) port
olive oil
salt and pepper
plain flour
1 × 440 ml can draught Guinness
570 ml (1 pint) chicken stock
450 g (1 lb) cooked and shelled
chestnuts

METHOD: Combine the venison, hare, wine, carrots, celery, onions, garlic, bay leaves, port, 5 tablespoons of olive oil and a generous seasoning of pepper in a bowl. Cover and set aside overnight.

Remove the meat from the marinade, pat dry and toss in seasoned flour. Fry in olive oil until lightly coloured. Add the Guinness, marinade, chicken stock, salt and pepper and the vegetables and cook for 1 hour, covered, or until tender.

Remove the meat, and reduce the sauce over a high heat for 15 minutes. Liquidise the sauce and push through a sieve. Replace the meat, add the chestnuts and reheat gently before serving with mash and red cabbage or turnips.

BAKED GUINEA FOWL WITH
CHICORY AND BALSAMIC VINEGAR

Guinea fowl, much loved by the French, are gaining in popularity here and can be found in most good butchers and supermarkets. According to one story, the sisters of the Greek poet Meleager wept so much on his death that Artemis changed them into guinea fowl – their tears are the white speckles on the bird's plumage.

It is best to do this recipe with the legs of the bird and reserve the breasts for separate treatment, but if you are going to cook the breasts in the same way, take them out 5 minutes earlier. The remainder of the carcass can be used as the basis of a stock.

SERVES 2

2 legs and thighs, attached, from a guinea fowl
olive oil
salt and pepper

1 garlic clove
2 heads of chicory
bunch of thyme
balsamic vinegar

METHOD: Preheat the oven to gas mark 6/400°F/200°C.

In a shallow frying pan lightly colour the guinea fowl in 2 tablespoons of olive oil. Remove, pat dry and season well with salt and pepper. Rub the cut side of the garlic clove into the meat. Blanch the chicory in boiling water for 2 minutes, drain and refresh under cold water and gently squeeze out any excess moisture. Cut each chicory head into quarters lengthways.

Arrange the guinea fowl on 2 pieces of tin foil, put the chicory on top and add a sprinkling of thyme and 1 tablespoon of balsamic vinegar per portion. Wrap up the tin foil parcels and bake in a roasting tray for 20 minutes, or until the meat is tender.

ROAST GUINEA FOWL
WITH PUY LENTILS

Tiny, perfectly formed and the most engaging slate blue-grey, Puy lentils stand as the undisputed emperor of the lentil kingdom. I will eat them hot, cold, warm, mashed, whole, accompanied, single, with a fork and, during occasional moments of desperation, squashed between hunks of bread. I am addicted, guilty of an irrational passion, and the curious thing is, I can't really explain why: the colour, texture, shape, flavour? None of these fully explains why a plate of these humble but simply delicious pulses will have me curled up in the corner, bowl in hands, positively hostile to any sort of interruption.

SERVES 4

1 lemon
1 guinea fowl
bunch of tarragon
2 garlic cloves, unpeeled
50 g (2 oz) butter
salt and pepper
1 glass white wine

1 small onion, peeled and finely
  chopped
olive oil
50 g (2 oz) smoked streaky bacon,
  finely chopped
175 g (6 oz) Puy lentils

METHOD: Preheat the oven to gas mark 7/425°F/220°C.

Cut the lemon up and stuff into the cavity of the bird, along with the tarragon and garlic. Smear the outside of the bird with the butter – using your hands is the easiest way to do this – and season well with salt and pepper. Put in a roasting tin in the oven for 15 minutes. Baste and pour in the wine, return to the oven, lower the temperature to gas mark 6/400°F/ 200°C and roast for 30 minutes. Turn the oven off, leave the door open and allow the guinea fowl to rest for 10 minutes.

While the guinea fowl is roasting, sauté the onion in 2 tablespoons of olive oil for 10 minutes without colouring. Add the bacon and continue cooking for 2 minutes. Add the lentils and coat thoroughly in the oil. Pour over 275 ml (½ pint) of water, bring to the boil for 10 minutes, lower the heat and simmer for 30 minutes, or until tender.

Remove the guinea fowl to a carving board or plate and pour the lentils into the roasting tin. Boil off any excess liquid over a moderate heat and serve with the guinea fowl, sliced.

PARTRIDGE WITH GRAPE AND PINE NUT STUFFING AND HASSELBACK POTATOES

This recipe actually works better if the grapes are unripe, its original inspiration coming as it does from the use of verjuice, an acidic juice extracted from large unripened grapes. This was widely used as a sauce ingredient, condiment and for deglazing, but has dropped out of favour and is not easily obtainable. The sourness works well with the sweet undertones of the partridge.

SERVES 4

8 medium potatoes
110 g (4 oz) butter
olive oil
salt and pepper
8 garlic cloves, unpeeled
2 tablespoons pine nuts

110 g (4 oz) seedless green grapes,
  halved
juice of ½ a lemon
4 partridges
175 ml (6 fl oz) white wine

METHOD: Preheat the oven to gas mark 6/400°F/200°C.

Peel the potatoes and cut vertical slices at ½ cm (¼ inch) intervals almost but not quite the whole way through the potato. I find the easiest way to do this is by putting a skewer either side of the potatoes, so the knife doesn't cut through. Rinse thoroughly in cold water and set in a roasting tray. Dot with half the butter, dribble over 4 tablespoons of olive oil, season with salt and pepper, scatter the garlic cloves around the potatoes and roast in the preheated oven for 1 hour, basting 3 or 4 times.

Gently roast the pine nuts in a dry frying pan over a high heat until just coloured. Combine with the grapes and lemon juice, season with salt and pepper and stuff the partridges. Rub the remaining butter into the skin of the partridges and add to the potatoes, for the last 30 minutes, which should be sufficient to cook the partridge. Remove and allow to rest for 10 minutes. Deglaze the pan with the white wine, allow to reduce by half and serve with the potatoes, which should have a crisp top to them.

STEAMED PHEASANT WITH CHESTNUTS, CABBAGE AND GINGER

The smell of roasting pheasants is one of autumn's delights. The game season is in full swing, gone is that rather regretful mood that summer is over, there's a whole new season opening up. Much as I adore the smell, roasting a pheasant can leave you with dry meat. Careful basting is the only answer, but it does rather tie you to the kitchen. Steaming is a successful alternative, keeping the meat moist and, in this recipe, allowing all the cooking to be done in one pot.

SERVES 4

4 pheasant breasts
olive oil
1 Savoy cabbage
salt and pepper
about 20 peeled chestnuts
5 cm (2 inch) piece of ginger,
  peeled and cut into matchstick
  strips

1 hard-boiled egg, roughly chopped
1 tablespoon capers, gently squeezed
  and roughly chopped
1 teaspoon Dijon mustard
8 gherkins, finely chopped

METHOD: Sauté the pheasant in olive oil on both sides briefly. In the bottom of your steamer blanch the outer leaves of the cabbage in boiling salted water for 2 minutes, remove, refresh under cold water and pat dry. Season each pheasant breast with salt and pepper, dribble over a tablespoon of olive oil, wrap in a cabbage leaf, and secure with a cocktail stick. Core and slice the remainder of the cabbage. In the top of the steamer put the cabbage, chestnuts and the ginger and season with salt and pepper. Lay the pheasant parcels on top and steam for 20 minutes, or until the pheasant is cooked.

Combine the egg, capers, mustard and gherkins with enough olive oil to form a thick sauce. Arrange the cabbage mixture on 4 plates, cut each pheasant parcel into 4 slices and put on top of the cabbage. Dribble over a little of the sauce and serve.

PHEASANT BRAISED WITH
CIDER, APPLES AND GINGER

I eat a lot of pheasant throughout the autumn and winter months and although there are endless recipes it is this one to which I return most often. Perhaps it is the connection with northern France, with all that Calvados, cream, cider and butter. The end result can be as rough or as fine as you like. If I'm feeling lazy, I just whisk in a little cream at the end and leave the vegetables whole. This also works well as a dish to cook for entertaining. You do all the carving, lay the slices in a shallow dish and cover with the sauce. Reheat gently and serve.

SERVES 4

5 cm (2 inch) piece of ginger, peeled and roughly chopped
2 pheasant
oil for frying
110 ml (4 fl oz) Calvados
50 g (2 oz) butter
6 leeks, trimmed and cleaned but left whole

2 eating apples (Cox's are best), cored and roughly chopped
salt and pepper
275 ml (½ pint) cider
110 ml (4 fl oz) double cream

METHOD: Divide the ginger in half and put inside the cavity of each bird. Heat 3 tablespoons of oil in a casserole large enough to take all the ingredients and colour the birds lightly. Remove the pheasant and discard the oil. Return the birds and the pot to the heat, pour over the Calvados and when it boils, set light to it. As soon as the flames have settled down, add the butter, the leeks and the apples to the casserole. Season everything with salt and pepper, cover with tin foil and then the lid and simmer over a moderate heat for 20 minutes, basting at least 2 or 3 times.

After 20 minutes add the cider. Continue to cook for a further 20 minutes, again basting at least 2 or 3 times. Remove the pheasant and allow to rest. Push the mixture through a sieve into a clean saucepan and stir in the cream. Simmer until the sauce thickens and serve with the pheasant.

GRILLED PIGEON WITH
GAME JUS AND GARLIC MASH

It took me quite some time to work out why pigeons in restaurants tasted sweeter, were more succulent and seemed to have more meat on them than the ones I bought to cook at home. The pigeons served up in restaurants are usually 'squabs'. Reared for the table, they are often corn-fed and are reliably moist and succulent – they also cost a bit more than their wild brothers (see the next recipe). Wood pigeon, on the other hand, have a good gamy taste and are relatively cheap. Flashed under the grill, the breasts remain tender and make quite a feast if served up with a jus made from the rest of the bird.

SERVES 4

4 large pigeons	*2 garlic cloves, roughly chopped*
juice of 1 lemon	*570 ml (1 pint) red wine*
olive oil	*150 ml (5 fl oz) double cream*
salt and pepper	*175 ml (6 fl oz) milk*
2 carrots, peeled and finely chopped	*900 g (2 lb) potatoes, cooked and*
2 sticks of celery, finely chopped	*mashed (this can be cold)*
1 onion, peeled and finely chopped	*50 g (2 oz) grated Parmesan*

METHOD: Remove the breasts from the pigeons, leaving the skin on, by sliding a sharp knife down each side of the breastbone and easing the meat away. Transfer to a bowl, cover with the lemon juice, 5 tablespoons of olive oil and a seasoning of salt and pepper. Roughly cut up all the remaining carcasses with kitchen scissors or a heavy knife and brown in a heavy casserole with a further 5 tablespoons of olive oil, the carrots, celery, onion and garlic, for 10 minutes. Pour over the wine and 175 ml (6 fl oz) of water and reduce until you have about 2 cupfuls, about 20 minutes. Strain into a clean saucepan, pushing as much of the juice through as you can, and set aside.

Combine the cream and milk with 5 tablespoons of olive oil in a saucepan and heat until just beginning to bubble. Whisk in the mash, adding a little more milk if it looks too stiff. Finally whisk in the Parmesan, remove from the heat and cover with a tea towel.

Preheat the grill, arrange the breasts on a wire tray and grill for 4–5 minutes on each side, or until just coloured. Serve on top of the mash with a little of the sauce on the side.

148

SQUAB WITH RED WINE SAUCE
AND CELERIAC MASH

What we see in restaurants today will be on our tables tomorrow. So has polenta crept into our kitchens, along with mash, risotto, sticky toffee pudding (actually an old friend returned), rocket and sun-dried tomatoes. Squab, the next in line, are pigeon bred for the table with a sweet, slightly gamy flavour and lots of meat. On the whole, farmed meat gets a thumbs down from me, but there are exceptions – venison is one (see meat chapter) and squab are definitely another. You may need to order them in advance, but your butcher should have no problem obtaining them provided he is given enough warning.

SERVES 4

4 squab	*275 ml (½ pint) red wine*
olive oil	*salt and pepper*
2 carrots, roughly chopped	*1 large or 2 small celeriac*
2 sticks celery, roughly chopped	*50 g (2 oz) butter*
1 onion, roughly chopped	

METHOD: Preheat the oven to gas mark 6/400°F/200°C.

Remove the legs and breasts from the birds with a sharp knife. Roughly chop the carcasses and colour in 4 tablespoons of olive oil with the carrots, celery and onion for 10 minutes. Pour off any excess oil and pour in the red wine. Reduce over a moderate heat until syrupy. Add 275 ml (½ pint) of water, bring to the boil and reduce by half. Strain and set aside, discarding the detritus.

Lightly colour the squab legs and breasts in 2 tablespoons of olive oil, season with salt and pepper and transfer to the oven. Roast for 20–25 minutes. Remove and allow to rest for at least 5 minutes. Peel and cut the celeriac into 2.5 cm (1 inch) chunks. Cook in boiling salted water for 10 minutes or until just tender, drain, liquidise and push through a sieve. Whisk the butter into the celeriac, season with salt and pepper and keep warm.

Remove the meat from the breastbones of the squab, slice diagonally and serve with the legs, the celeriac mash and the red wine sauce, gently reheated.

POACHED POUSSIN AND
ROOT VEGETABLES WITH AÏOLI

You can't mess about with aïoli sauce: smooth, glistening yellow mayonnaise laced with garlic – it can raise the hairs on the back of your neck, and I know some who simply refuse to eat it. But what a feast they are missing! This is food that demands attention, is guaranteed to raise the spirits and push even the worst of days into the background. Kept in one of those sealed preserving jars, this sauce – there is more than you will need – will keep in the fridge for at least a week, perfect for scooping up with a raw carrot when you fall through the door in need of a little restoring. Originally aïoli was just garlic and oil, but modern versions usually incorporate the egg yolks.

SERVES 4

2 poussins	*4 carrots, trimmed and peeled*
2 small onions	*4 small turnips, trimmed and peeled*
8 peppercorns	*4 garlic cloves, peeled*
2 bay leaves	*3 egg yolks*
bunch of parsley	*275 ml (½ pint) olive oil*
salt and pepper	*275 ml (½ pint) vegetable oil*
4 leeks, trimmed and washed	*1 lemon*

METHOD: Put the onions inside the poussins and put the birds in a casserole large enough to accomodate the vegetables later. Add the peppercorns, bay leaves and the stems from the parsley, tied together, plus a seasoning of salt, and cover with cold water. Put the lid on and slowly bring to the boil, skimming off any froth that floats to the surface. Lower the heat and simmer at the gentlest setting for 15 minutes. Add the trimmed vegetables and cook for a further 25 minutes at the same setting.

Meanwhile make the aïoli. My own favoured utensil is a pestle and mortar, the weight of the former making the stirring easier, but a bowl and wooden spoon can be used. The garlic must be pounded to a pulp and then incorporated with the egg yolks. Mix the two oils together – all olive oil makes it too rich – and add, drop by drop at first and then in a steady stream. If the sauce splits take a clean bowl, a new egg yolk and gradually add your mixture and then the rest of the oil. Season with lemon juice and salt at the end to taste. Serve with the poussin and vegetables and a sprinkling of parsley. The stock can then be used for soup.

GRILLED SPATCHCOCKED QUAIL WITH MUSHROOM CROSTINI

After ordering quail one year in France I was more than a little surprised to have the entire bird – minus its feet – served up on my plate. It was a village restaurant and we were paying a mere 80F for four courses; even so, I wouldn't have objected if a little more carving had been done prior to delivery. The quail we get in this country are ideal for spatchcocking, cleaned as they are from top to bottom. A good pair of kitchen scissors and the job is completed in minutes.

SERVES 4

8 quail
salt and pepper
1 teaspoon finely chopped rosemary
olive oil
2 lemons

225 g (½ lb) large flat mushrooms,
wiped clean and finely chopped
2 garlic cloves, peeled and finely
chopped
half stick French bread

METHOD: Turn the quail so they are breast down and with a pair of scissors cut along both sides of the backbone. Discard the backbone, rinse the quail under cold water and press flat. Insert a skewer through each thigh to keep them flat and transfer to a bowl. Season with salt and pepper, sprinkle over the rosemary, 110 ml (4 fl oz) of olive oil and the juice and roughly chopped skin of the lemons. Mix everything well and set aside for as long as possible, or overnight in the fridge.

Remove the quail from the marinade and arrange on a wire rack for the grill. Remove the lemon pieces from the marinade and pour the marinade into a saucepan with the mushrooms and garlic. Cover with a lid, toss over a high heat for 2 minutes, reduce the heat and sweat for 10 minutes, or until the mushrooms are tender. Cut the bread into thin slices, brush with olive oil and grill on both sides until golden; set aside.

Grill the quail, breast side away from the heat, for 5 minutes. Turn over and grill for a further 8 minutes, or until the skin is golden brown and the flesh cooked. Put the quail on to a serving plate, spoon the mushrooms on to the slices of bread with a little of the juice and serve alongside the quail.

STUFFED QUAIL WITH
WATERCRESS SALAD

It seems surprising given quails' tiny size, but the ancient Greeks and Romans are supposed to have used them for fighting much as they did cocks, the quail having a fierce temper. We know quail as a farmed creature, popping up on supermarket shelves wrapped in plastic, but there are wild cousins – although the breeding population in Britain and Ireland is tiny, so small that the bird is protected. The farmed version, however, is ideal for marinating or stuffing. Indeed, they seem almost made for the latter with a sufficiently large cavity. You can bone out quail quite easily, but I think half the fun is in laying down your knife and fork and getting stuck in – perfect finger food.

SERVES 4

110 g (4 oz) chicken livers
olive oil
1 shallot, finely chopped
1 stick celery, finely chopped
110 g (4 oz) mushrooms, wiped and
*   roughly chopped*
1 garlic clove, peeled and finely chopped

2 tablespoons breadcrumbs
salt and pepper
8 quail
50 g (2 oz) butter
4 handfuls of watercress
red wine vinegar

METHOD: Preheat the oven to gas mark 5/375°F/190°C.

Lightly fry the chicken livers in 2 tablespoons of olive oil for 2 minutes. Remove, allow to cool and roughly chop. Put in a bowl along with any juices. Add the shallot and celery to the hot oil and gently sauté for 5 minutes, without colouring. Add the mushrooms and, 2 minutes later, the garlic. Continue cooking until the mushrooms release their juices, 3 or 4 minutes. Add the breadcrumbs, coat in the oil, combine with the livers and season with salt and pepper.

When the mixture is cool enough to handle, stuff each of the quail, then retie the legs to seal the cavity. Rub the butter into the outside of the birds and season well with salt and pepper. Roast the birds for 20 minutes, basting once or twice.

Toss the watercress in 3 tablespoons of olive oil, season with salt and pepper and add a teaspoon of vinegar. Toss well and serve the quail on top.

Pot-roasted salmon
with capers and black olives
(*page 117*)

Chicken 'satay' with pickled chillies and vegetable noodles *(page 130)*

Grilled spatchcocked quail with mushroom crostini *(page 151)*

Lamb brochettes with couscous salad and spiced yoghurt *(page 161)*

Beef and stout stew with garlic mash (*page 175*)

Italian sausages with wilted greens, whole garlic and thyme *(page 178)*

Grilled pink grapefruit with saffron and honey cream *(page 204)*

Plum charlottes with cinnamon cream *(page 205)*

ROAST RABBIT WITH
PANCETTA AND LIME BUTTER

Throughout mainland Europe rabbit is highly regarded while we seem to shun it, perhaps because of associations with past war-time necessity, or possibly with thoughts of Beatrix Potter and her well-loved tales of Peter Rabbit. However, rabbit does make for excellent eating and if you can overcome any initial reluctance you'll find it is also quite cheap. Supermarkets now sell ready packed portions of rabbit which are ideally suited to this recipe. Rabbit doesn't contain much fat, hence the pancetta overcoat, but basting during cooking is also important if you want to ensure the meat stays moist.

SERVES 4

8 rabbit pieces	175 g (6 oz) butter
salt and pepper	2 limes
bunch of thyme	6 sun-dried tomatoes, roughly chopped
1 garlic clove, peeled and finely chopped	
8 slices pancetta (or unsmoked streaky bacon)	

METHOD: Preheat the oven to gas mark 6/400°F/200°C.

Season the rabbit pieces with salt and pepper, sprinkle over a little thyme and garlic and wrap in the pancetta, securing with a cocktail stick. Arrange in a roasting tin.

Melt the butter in a saucepan, draw off the heat and when the white solids have dropped to the bottom pour the clarified butter over the rabbit pieces. Roast for 30 minutes, basting once or twice during that time.

Remove the rabbit pieces and allow to rest in the switched off oven for 10 minutes with the door open. Put the roasting tray over a moderate heat and add the juice and the zest from the limes to the butter along with the tomatoes. Serve the rabbit with the lime butter and tomatoes.

RABBIT STEW WITH PINE NUT
AND PARSLEY DUMPLINGS

Dumplings seem to have slipped out of fashion a bit, their association with boiled beef and carrots and long-simmered stews somehow not fitting into our current liking for fast, straightforward food. This is a pity: not only are they delicious, but a distinct advantage for me is that they cook in the same pot. As well as saving on washing up, it means you can leave things to look after themselves.

SERVES 4

2 dessertspoons pine nuts
3 tablespoons finely chopped parsley
50 g (2 oz) self-raising flour, sifted
50 g (2 oz) breadcrumbs
50 g (2 oz) shredded suet
salt and pepper
1 egg
12 baby onions, peeled

110 g (4 oz) pork belly in a piece
olive oil
8 rabbit portions
1 glass brandy
275 ml (½ pint) white wine
275 ml (½ pint) rabbit or chicken
stock
bunch of thyme

METHOD: Dry roast the pine nuts in a hot frying pan until just coloured. Combine with the parsley, flour, breadcrumbs, suet and a generous seasoning of salt and pepper. Beat in the egg and shape into 8 dumplings using a teaspoon.

Brown the onions and pork in 5 tablespoons of olive oil for 5 minutes, add the rabbit and continue to sauté for 2 minutes, turning the rabbit so it is gently coloured. Pour in the brandy and set alight. When the flames have died down, season with salt and pepper and pour in the wine. Allow to reduce for 5 minutes, then add the stock and the dumplings and gently simmer, covered, for 1 hour or until cooked. Remove the pork, stir in a handful of thyme leaves and serve.

Meat

Whether it's the sheer pleasure of Aberdeen Angus beef, the salty tang of west-coast lamb, the rich succulence of pork or the delights of Scottish venison – our climate, soil and farming methods produce meat that is the envy of the world. With such superb ingredients, is it any wonder we enjoy dishes like steak and kidney pudding, roast beef, hot-pots and casseroles, or the summer delights of grilled chops or our beloved bangers cooked on a barbecue?

The glories of meat eating have been somewhat overshadowed in recent years by concern over farming practices and the realisation that as a nation we rely too heavily on meat, a source of much pleasure for many but also rich in unwanted saturated fat. Like so many people, my meat consumption has fallen over the years, but I still enjoy it and the following recipes are some favourites.

Fat may be unwanted, but there is much evidence to suggest that a lot of the flavour actually comes from the fat. I may not eat beef that often, but when I do I buy it with thick yellow fat which runs right through the meat, ensuring it stays moist and full of flavour.

The growing band of small producers selling organic, free-range or so-called real meat has led to an overall increase in quality and also reflects a growing awareness and concern by the consumer of the reality of modern farming practices. Tethered animals, light bulbs and large overcrowded sheds contrast unpleasantly with our image of free move-ment, daylight and fresh grass, but this is the unfortunate reality for much of what we eat. The movement back to small-scale farming without the unquestioning use of chemicals is one of the most exciting developments of recent years and it is helping to formulate the super-markets' approach as well. Following consumer demand, they are becoming much more aware of the welfare issues involved in meat, and of the need to increase quality.

Schemes under which meat is produced following certain guidelines may reassure us, but bear in mind that many are self-regulatory. Organic, free-range and so-called real meat are all to be welcomed, but it is as well to be aware that the terms can sometimes be used as a marketing tool, part of which is designed to make you pay more for what you are getting. The small print is important and any one of the many high-quality producers should meet any questions you might have with enthusiasm. It should be of as much interest to them as it is to you to make sure you are satisfied and happy about what you intend buying.

Taste, texture and flavour are dependent on so many variable factors in meat production: how the animals are fed and cared for, the conditions and methods of slaughter, and how good your butcher is. Butchery is a skill that takes years to acquire and develop, and while the standard of butchery in supermarkets is good, they are of necessity producing a streamlined succession of products which must reach a certain level of sales to find their way on to the shelves. Not so with the high street butcher, who buys in whole carcasses and must make use of the whole thing as he has no one else to sell leftovers on to. I am not suggesting that every high street butcher is good, far from it, but those that are sell more than just meat. They will often make their own black pudding, marinate cuts for barbecuing, cut to order, make their own sausages, supply fresh offal and ensure that what they do sell will satisfy you. And if it doesn't, tell them.

One aspect of cooking meat that is often overlooked is the importance of allowing it to rest. This is essential with roast, grilled and fried meat, but also with stews and casseroles, which will taste better the following day when all the flavours have been allowed to develop. Toughness and dryness are often the result of not allowing the meat to relax and the juices to run.

BAKED LAMB WITH BLACK OLIVES, WHITE WINE AND SAGE

New-season's lamb in the spring and early summer is one of the real treats of our climate. If you are lucky, your butcher will follow the season up through the country, buying his meat initially from Devon or Cornwall and eventually from wind-swept Scotland. In each area it is different and while some extol the benefits of herb-infused lowland lamb, my favourite is the salty tang of lamb that has fed on grasses near the sea.

SERVES 4

2 red onions, peeled and sliced
4 carrots, peeled and finely chopped
olive oil
700 g (1½ lb) shoulder of lamb, cubed
275 ml (½ pint) white wine
275 ml (½ pint) chicken stock

1 head of garlic, split into cloves and peeled
225 g (½ lb) pitted black olives
bunch of sage
1 bay leaf
2 tablespoons chopped parsley
salt and pepper

METHOD: Preheat the oven to gas mark 4/350°F/180°C.

Soften the onion and carrots in 3 tablespoons of olive oil for 10 minutes without colouring and set aside. Brown the meat in batches; you may require a little more olive oil. Pour off any excess fat, return the pan to the heat and deglaze with the white wine and stock.

Blanch the garlic in boiling water for 1 minute and refresh under cold water. Put the olives, garlic, meat, onion and carrot in a gratin dish. Add a few sprigs of sage, the bay leaf and the parsley, season with salt and pepper and pour over the white wine and stock. Cover with tin foil and bake for 45 minutes. Uncover and continue cooking for a further 30 minutes, or until the meat is done.

LOIN OF LAMB CHOPS WITH SHERRY VINEGAR SAUCE AND SAUTÉED POTATOES

Wine vinegar, whether it is sherry, red or white wine, has been somewhat elbowed aside by our enthusiasm for balsamic vinegar. Fond as I am of this Italian ingredient, it often lacks subtlety, unless that is, you can afford to buy the well-aged versions and then you are unlikely to want to splash them into a hot pan. Wine vinegars have as much finesse and the sherry vinegar in this recipe imparts a delicate sharpness to the lamb.

SERVES 4

900 g (2 lb) potatoes	*4 loin of lamb chops*
olive oil for frying	*3 tablespoons sherry vinegar*
2 teaspoons finely chopped rosemary	*1 glass red wine*
salt and pepper	*150 ml (5 fl oz) chicken stock*

METHOD: Cut the potatoes into cubes, about the same size as a dice. Heat 5 tablespoons of olive oil in a shallow pan and when hot, slide in the potatoes. Don't touch them for the first 3 minutes, then gently toss them so they brown evenly, for 5–10 minutes, or until cooked. Two minutes before they are done, add the rosemary, salt and a generous seasoning of freshly ground black pepper.

Meanwhile fry the chops in a lightly oiled frying pan until done to your liking, about 3–4 minutes each side for medium. Remove and keep warm. Tip off any excess fat and add the sherry vinegar, red wine and stock. Reduce by about half, check seasoning and serve with the chops and potatoes.

LEG OF LAMB STEAKS WITH GRILLED MEDITERRANEAN VEGETABLES AND BALSAMIC VINEGAR

We more normally associate leg of lamb with a large roasting joint, but any good butcher will remove the bone – no easy task – and cut you thin steaks which are ideal for barbecuing, grilling or frying. This cut is also proving increasingly popular in supermarkets. That way you get all the flavour of that particular cut, but don't have to spend the time roasting an entire leg. Alternatively, do as the Spanish and Italians do and buy your lamb really young so the legs are small. A hot oven and a few herbs will have the meat moist and succulent in a very short time.

SERVES 4

4 leg of lamb steaks, about 1 cm (½ inch) thick
1 garlic clove, cut in half
2 red peppers
2 aubergines

4 courgettes
olive oil
balsamic vinegar
salt and pepper

METHOD: Rub the lamb on both sides with the garlic clove and set aside. Grill the peppers whole until the skins become black – the blacker the better. Transfer to a bowl and cover with cling film. Slice the aubergines and courgettes lengthways and grill until charred slightly. Remove to a bowl, pour over 5 tablespoons of olive oil, 2 tablespoons of vinegar and a seasoning of salt and pepper while still warm.

When the peppers are cool enough to handle peel the charred skin and discard. If you are in a hurry do this under a cold tap to save your fingers. Arrange the grilled vegetables on 4 plates, grill the steaks to your liking – 3 minutes each side for rare, 5 minutes for well done; in both cases allow to rest for 5 minutes – and serve on top of the vegetables with a seasoning of salt and pepper.

LAMB BROCHETTES
WITH COUSCOUS SALAD
AND SPICED YOGHURT

When I'm feeling efficient I prepare these brochettes the night before and leave them marinating in the fridge, where the flavours of garlic, lemon and thyme mingle with the meat. Usually, though, they get as much time as I can spare having arrived home with the ingredients, which can be as little as 20 minutes, so I keep tossing them in the marinade periodically. Even when I do the rushed version, I still adore the colour and the flavour, there is lots of crunch and it's a good excuse to use your fingers to eat with. You will need wooden satay sticks, which are available in most, but not all supermarkets. Alternative sources are hardware stores.

SERVES 4

1 yellow and 1 red pepper	3 lemons
1 red onion	bunch of coriander
2 courgettes	175 ml (6 fl oz) yoghurt
450 g (1 lb) shoulder of lamb, cut into cubes	425 ml (15 fl oz) couscous
bunch of thyme	bunch of spring onions, finely chopped
2 garlic cloves, finely chopped	1 cucumber, diced
olive oil	bunch of radishes, finely sliced
salt and pepper	

METHOD: Cut the peppers, red onion and courgettes into cubes and thread on to wooden satay sticks, putting a piece of meat between each vegetable. Put in a bowl along with a generous quantity of the thyme leaves, the garlic, 75 ml (3 fl oz) of olive oil, salt and pepper and the juice and skin from two of the lemons. The skin can be roughly chopped. Toss all this in the bowl and set aside.

Remove the coriander leaves from the stalks, put in a bowl of ice-cold water and set aside. Finely chop the stalks and add these, along with a generous seasoning of salt and pepper, to the yoghurt and set aside.

Add 425 ml (15 fl oz) of boiling water to the couscous and set aside with a towel over it for 10 minutes. Toss the couscous with a fork and add the spring onion, cucumber, radishes and reserved coriander leaves. Season generously with salt and pepper, add 5 tablespoons of olive oil and the juice of the remaining lemon and toss together with a fork.

Preheat the grill and cook the brochettes for 3–5 minutes each side. Serve on top of the couscous with a generous dollop of yoghurt on the side and a sprinkling of the coriander leaves.

Provided you add the same quantity by volume of boiling water to couscous, the grains will cook in 10 minutes under a towel – far easier than all that steaming.

SHOULDER OF LAMB
WITH ROAST SPRING VEGETABLES

Sweet, succulent and packed with flavour, shoulder is one of my favourite cuts of lamb. It's more usually boned and then stuffed, but I prefer to roast it with the bone in. Carving is a little tricky, but only if you are in search of those large smooth slices that you get from a leg. Here the slices are smaller, but they are more than compensated for by the flavour. Served on top of a mound of caramelised vegetables this is a real spring-time feast.

SERVES 4

1 × 1¾ kg (4 lb) shoulder of lamb	*1 head of celery*
salt and pepper	*6 turnips*
6 bay leaves	*12 baby carrots*
3 small globe artichokes (there is no	*3 red onions*
need to remove the spiky/hairy bits	*3 chicory*
if they are young)	*3 tablespoons chopped parsley*

METHOD: Preheat the oven to gas mark 7/425°F/220°C.

Season the meat with salt and pepper and put on top of the bay leaves and garlic in a roasting tin – no need to peel the garlic. Roast in the oven for 20 minutes and then add 175 ml (6 fl oz) of water, lower the temperature to gas mark 5/375°F/190°C and continue cooking the lamb for a further 50–60 minutes. Remove the lamb to a plate and allow to rest in a warm place for at least 15 minutes and return the oven to the original setting.

Meanwhile blanch the vegetables in a pan of salted water as follows: the artichokes, cut in quarters (stems removed) for 3 minutes; the celery, cut into 6 lengthways, for 2 minutes; the turnips, cut into halves, for 2 minutes; and the carrots for 3 minutes. In all cases refresh under cold water and pat dry. Peel and cut the red onions into quarters, and likewise the chicory – these do not need blanching.

Drain off all but 2 tablespoons of fat from the roasting tin, add the vegetables and toss so they are well coated. Season with salt and pepper and put at the top of the oven for 20 minutes, until cooked, brown and bubbling.

Serve the meat on top of the vegetables with a generous sprinkling of parsley.

ROAST SHOULDER OF LAMB
WITH GREEN BEANS AND
SUN-DRIED TOMATO DRESSING

Towards the end of the summer, when tomatoes are good, plentiful and cheap, you can try this alternative to sun-dried tomatoes. Cut the tomatoes in half, sprinkle over a little salt and bake them on a rack in the lowest oven possible for about 4 hours. Not as intense as the sun-dried variety, they are delicious in salads, or with grilled meats.

SERVES 6

1 × 1¾ kg (4 lb) shoulder of lamb   *450 g (1 lb) green beans, trimmed*
salt and pepper   *4 sun-dried tomato halves*
4 garlic cloves, unpeeled   *olive oil*
bunch of rosemary   *lemon juice*
1 glass white wine

METHOD: Preheat the oven to gas mark 7/425°F/220°C.

Season the meat with salt and pepper. Put the garlic in the bottom of a roasting tin, put a few sprigs of rosemary on top and then the meat. Place in the oven and roast for 20 minutes. Reduce the temperature to gas mark 3/375°F/190°C and pour the wine and an equal quantity of water into the tin. Return the tin to the oven and continue cooking for 50–60 minutes. Transfer the meat to a plate and leave in the switched off oven with the door open.

Cook the beans in boiling salted water until almost done. Refresh under cold water and then add to the roasting tin, coating the beans with the juices over a low heat. Finely chop the sun-dried tomatoes and mix with 5 tablespoons of olive oil, a seasoning of salt and pepper and lemon juice to taste.

Serve the meat on top of the beans with a generous dribbling of the dressing.

NOISETTES OF LAMB WITH
BAKED PARSNIPS AND
TOMATO RELISH

I don't know if it is that melt-in-the-mouth texture, or their natural sweetness, but parsnips come high on my list of desert island vegetables. The
Romans used to like them, and are supposed to have matched them with
honey and fruit for dessert. In the Middle Ages babies were given them in
place of dummies to suck on (lucky babies – all you get today is a bit of
rubberised plastic). So popular was the parsnip it appeared at many meals
until the arrival of the potato, whose versatility made it more widespread.

Relish too often means something simmered for hours and bottled, or
some ready-made confection plucked from the shelf. Indian cuisine is full
of relishes quickly prepared when other dishes are simmering. They have a
fresh vibrancy which is appealing and, thankfully, not overpowering.

SERVES 4

8 tomatoes, peeled, deseeded and cut into quarters	*5 tablespoons vinegar*
	salt and pepper
1 red pepper, deseeded and chopped	*8 parsnips*
25 g (1 oz) sugar	*olive oil*
1 teaspoon mustard seeds	*4 noisettes of lamb*

METHOD: Preheat the oven to gas mark 7/425°F/220°C.

Put the tomatoes, pepper, sugar, mustard seeds and vinegar into a
saucepan, season with salt and pepper, bring to the boil and simmer for 2
minutes. Remove from the heat and allow to cool.

Peel and trim the parsnips and blanch in boiling salted water for 2
minutes. Refresh under cold water and pat dry. Lightly toss the parsnips in
olive oil and roast at the top of the oven for 15 minutes, or until cooked.

Season the noisettes, fry or grill and serve with the parsnip and tomato
relish.

To peel tomatoes, drop into boiling water for 30 seconds, refresh under
cold water and peel.

LOIN OF LAMB WITH
AUBERGINE STUFFING AND
HARICOT AND ROSEMARY PURÉE

Loin of lamb is a perfect cut for stuffing, no wonder butchers are so keen to do it themselves. Buy the meat unstuffed, however, and there are all sorts of delicious things you can put inside to suit yourself. Lamb and aubergine is an all-year-round combination that I use again and again, sometimes with spices for a Moroccan flavour, sometimes without, as in this recipe. Make sure you use a cotton string to tie the meat up – nylon melts at a low temperature and doesn't add much to the flavour. If I remember I still prefer to soak my own beans (and they are cheaper), but the tinned versions do nicely when speed is necessary.

SERVES 6

2 aubergines	*1 garlic clove, peeled and finely chopped*
salt and pepper	*1 × 400 g (14 oz) tin of haricot*
lemon juice	*beans, drained and rinsed*
900 g (2 lb) loin of lamb, boned	*1 teaspoon finely chopped rosemary*
olive oil	*275 ml (½ pint) chicken stock*

METHOD: Preheat the oven to gas mark 6/400°F/200°C.

Prick the aubergines a few times with a fork and roast for 20 minutes until just soft. Cut in half lengthways and allow to cool. Scoop out the flesh and mash with a fork, then season with salt and pepper and lemon juice. Spread over the inside of the lamb, roll up and tie with string.

Reduce the oven temperature to gas mark 4/350°F/180°C. Lightly coat the outside of the meat with olive oil and roast in the oven for 1 hour 15 minutes (about 30 minutes, plus 20 minutes per pound).

When the meat has cooked, transfer to a plate and leave in the oven with door open and heat switched off. Skim any excess fat from the roasting pan and place over a moderate heat. Add the garlic, beans, the rosemary and chicken stock and simmer for 10 minutes. Purée, return to the pan, heat through and serve with slices of the meat. If the purée becomes too thick, loosen with a little water.

BAKED PORK WITH
NEW POTATOES AND FENNEL

The modern pig is very different from his ancestors and came about through a crossbreeding of Chinese and European pigs by Robert Bakewell, an Englishman, in the middle of the eighteenth century. Henceforth the common pig was a large beast kept by most families with a small bit of land throughout much of Europe and slaughtered in the autumn and early winter. First the offal, then the fresh meat, then the cured meat and sausages would find their way on to the table accompanied by dried beans, winter herbs, root vegetables, preserved fruits, vegetables and pickles. We rather lost the tradition in this country, the Industrial Revolution forcing us into cities where pigs were not welcome. This is changing, however, and there is now some wonderful pork on sale.

SERVES 4

700 g (1½ lb) diced pork
olive oil
2 heads of fennel
salt and pepper
4 garlic cloves, peeled and finely
*   chopped*

2 medium onions, peeled and cut into
*   thin half-moon slices*
150 ml (5 fl oz) chicken stock
225 ml (8 fl oz) dry white wine
2 bay leaves
450 g (1 lb) new potatoes
bunch of parsley

METHOD: Preheat the oven to gas mark 4/350°F/180°C.

Fry the meat in batches in olive oil until well browned. Drain and transfer to a shallow ovenproof dish large enough to take all the ingredients. Trim the fennel and cut, vertically, into thin slices. Blanch the fennel for 2 minutes in boiling salted water, refresh under cold water and add, along with the garlic, to the pork.

Lightly sauté the onion in the same frying pan you have cooked the meat in for 10–15 minutes without colouring and transfer to the dish. Deglaze the pan with the stock and wine, scraping up all the bits at the bottom of the pan. Pour this over the meat, insert the bay leaves and the new potatoes and bake, covered with foil, for 1 hour, removing the foil for the last 20 minutes. Sprinkle over the parsley and serve.

PORK FILLET WITH SESAME-SEED CRUST AND SWEET-CHILLI DRESSING

Sesame seeds add a gloriously nutty flavour when roasted which is dispro-portionate to their size. I now add them to carrot and cucumber salads, or sprinkle them over stir-fries and have been known, on occasion, to toast a few to eat as I cook. A dry frying pan is best for this, but watch it closely – toasted-to-burned takes but a few seconds.

SERVES 4

75 g (3 oz) sugar
3 kaffir lime leaves
1 stalk lemon grass
5 tablespoons Ketjap Manis
  (Indonesian soy sauce)
2 dessertspoons chilli sauce
soy sauce
fish sauce
1 lemon
1 yellow pepper

1 red onion
2 courgettes
1 dessertspoon each of chopped
  coriander and mint
1 pork fillet
plain flour
1 egg, lightly beaten
2 tablespoons sesame seeds
salt and pepper
oil for roasting

METHOD: In a saucepan, combine the sugar, 275 ml (½ pint) of water, the lime leaves, lemon grass cut into 2.5 cm (1 inch) pieces, the Ketjap Manis and chilli sauce. Bring to the boil and simmer for 5 minutes.

Remove from the heat and add a splash of soy sauce, 1 tablespoon of fish sauce and the juice of a lemon. Allow this mixture to cool.

Finely chop the yellow pepper and red onion. Trim the top and bottom from the courgette and cut into strips as thinly as possible – ideally they should be the thickness of matchsticks. Add these to the cooled syrup along with the coriander and mint. Refrigerate until required.

Preheat the oven to gas mark 6/400°F/200°C. Roll the pork in the flour, then in the egg and then in the sesame seeds and salt and pepper. Lightly oil a roasting tin, roll the meat in the oil and roast for 15 minutes. Allow to rest for a further 15 minutes in the turned off oven. Slice and serve with the dressing and some steamed broccoli.

THICK PORK CHOPS WITH
SPRING VEGETABLES

Years have been spent trying to breed out the fat from pork on the basis that we dislike this essential substance. The animal that was once a pig has been transformed into a lean machine and with the change pork has lost almost all texture and taste. But fear not, changes are afoot to return this humble creature to its rightful place, and guess what? Much effort is being put into breeding the fat back in again, a move that Britain is leading throughout Europe, along with the banning of tethered sows. Go forward with confidence and seek out a good butcher for he shall know good pork and distribute among the knowing.

SERVES 4

225 g (½ lb) asparagus, trimmed
225 g (½ lb) French beans, trimmed
4 heads of garlic
225 g (½ lb) baby carrots, trimmed
4 thick pork chops
olive oil

225 g (½ lb) broad beans, podded and
 peeled
225 g (½ lb) podded peas
1 glass white wine
bunch of fresh thyme

METHOD: Preheat the oven to gas mark 6/400°F/200°C.

Blanch the asparagus, French beans, unpeeled garlic and carrots in plenty of salted water for 2 minutes. Drain and refresh under cold water. Cut each head of garlic in two, across the cloves, so you end up with the exposed surface showing a cross-section of the cloves.

Lightly brown the pork chops in olive oil, add the garlic and roast in the oven for 30 minutes, or until the meat is cooked, basting at least twice during cooking. The garlic should be soft and creamy; if it is still hard roast for a little longer. Turn the oven off, transfer the chops and garlic to a plate and return to the oven, leaving the door open.

Transfer the blanched vegetables, with the broad beans and peas, to the pan. Add the white wine and an equal quantity of water and simmer over a moderate heat for 5 minutes, or until the vegetables are heated through.

Season with salt and pepper and sprinkle over a generous quantity of thyme. Serve with the meat and garlic.

Roast garlic loses all its astringent qualities and becomes moist and creamy.

POACHED PORK CHOPS
WITH SPICED CABBAGE

This recipe requires the now old-fashioned full-fat milk, which cooks down to a delicious creaminess at the end and keeps the chops moist and pale, a striking contrast with the dark red colour of the cabbage. I lived beside a farmer once who would bring a jug of milk to the back door on most evenings, fresh from his milking session. It was rich, strong, still frothing on top and almost warm, a wonderful treat.

SERVES 4

50 g (2 oz) butter
1 small red cabbage, cored and finely sliced
1 onion, peeled and finely chopped
1 teaspoon five-spice powder
1 glass cassis

salt and pepper
850 ml (1½ pints) milk
4 loin chops
2 teaspoons fennel seeds
6 peppercorns
1 bay leaf

METHOD: Melt the butter in a saucepan and sauté the red cabbage and onion for 5 minutes. Stir in the five-spice powder and continue to sauté for a further 5 minutes. Add the cassis, salt and pepper, cover and allow to cook over a low heat for 30 minutes, stirring every now and then.

In a shallow pan gently heat the milk, chops, fennel seeds, peppercorns, salt and bay leaf, making sure the chops do not stick to the bottom of the pan. Simmer for 10 minutes, turn the chops over and continue cooking for 10 minutes, or until tender. Remove the chops, brush off the milk solids and keep warm while you reduce the milk sauce for 5 minutes. Strain and serve with the chops, placing a dollop of the cabbage on top of the chops and the sauce at the side.

POACHED BACON WITH BUTTERED LENTILS AND SAUCE VIERGE

There is nothing to beat a piece of bacon: succulent, full of flavour and with almost no waste, it can provide one substantial meal and still leave you with enough to have cold the following day and a readymade stock for soup. In Ireland we traditionally eat it with colcannon, a creamy concoction of potatoes and cabbage but I prefer it this way with lentils.

SERVES 6–8

1.35 kg (3 lb) piece of bacon	*1 tablespoon finely chopped shallots*
2 onions	*2 tablespoons roughly chopped*
8 cloves	*gherkins*
4 carrots	*1 dessertspoon roughly chopped capers*
2 sticks celery	*2 tablespoons chopped parsley*
2 bay leaves	*75 g (3 oz) butter*
12 peppercorns	*3 spring onions, trimmed and finely*
450 g (1 lb) Puy lentils	*sliced*
olive oil	

METHOD: Place the bacon in a saucepan of cold water, bring to the boil and then pour off the boiling water together with any scum that collects on top. Put the bacon in a saucepan together with the onions (no need to peel them), studded with cloves, the carrots, celery, bay leaves and peppercorns. Cover with fresh water, slowly bring to the boil, lower the heat and simmer, covered, for 1 hour 15 minutes. Remove from the heat and leave to sit in the water for 10 minutes before serving.

Meanwhile sauté the lentils in 2 tablespoons of olive oil for 5 minutes. Pour in enough water to cover by 2.5 cm (1 inch) and simmer for 30–35 minutes, or until cooked. Drain and set aside. Combine the shallots, gherkins, capers, parsley and 3 tablespoons of olive oil.

When the bacon is cooked, melt the butter in a saucepan and gently reheat the lentils. Season with salt and pepper, stir in the spring onions and serve, with slices of bacon on top and a good spoonful of the sauce.

If you sauté lentils in olive oil before boiling them it helps to maintain their shape and gives them an attractive gloss.

171

POACHED BEEF WITH
ROOT VEGETABLES AND
MUSTARD FRUITS

Poaching is one of my favourite ways of cooking beef. It is so gentle, fills the kitchen with a sweet smell, is incredibly fast and provides the basis for another meal – the enriched stock at the end will form the basis of a wonderful soup or stew.

Mustard fruits (available from delicatessens and some supermarkets) originate in Italy: tiny fruits are poached in a syrup which is then infused with mustard. The result is both sweet and fiery. It is traditionally served with the Italian feast of bollito misto, a dish that requires hordes of people to make it worthwhile.

SERVES 6

900 g (2 lb) rump of beef in piece *4 carrots*
salt and pepper *12 baby onions*
1.75 litres (3 pints) beef stock *1 jar of mustard fruits*
4 parsnips

METHOD: If you have a griddle-pan with ridges, sear the meat on this; otherwise brown it under a very hot grill, or in a frying pan with a little olive oil. You don't want to cook the meat, just colour the outside. Season with salt and pepper and tie up with string as if it were a parcel. The meat needs to be suspended in the stock so you want the string to finish in the middle of the meat, or alternatively, have a string at either end.

Bring the stock to the boil, reduce the heat so it is barely simmering and lower the meat in. Tie the end of the string over a wooden spoon arranged across the top of the saucepan so the meat does not touch the bottom of the saucepan, but is covered by the stock. Poach the meat for 20 minutes, remove and keep warm.

Peel and cut the parsnips and carrots up into small batons, peel the onions and leave whole. While the meat is resting simmer the vegetables in the stock for 10 minutes, or until cooked. Slice the meat on the diagonal and serve with the vegetables and a little of the stock, and pass round the mustard fruits. Garlic mash is my passion with this; see page 175 for details.

STIR-FRIED BEEF WITH LEMON GRASS, COCONUT AND GINGER

Lemon grass is a wonderful ingredient and now widely available, although I have on occasion been sold rather tame versions with not much in the way of flavour. When split open, the inside should taste strongly of lemon, with more than a slight hint of chilli in the background. If you are testing in the shop, try squeezing and bending it a little – the lemon flavour should smell quite strong.

SERVES 4

vegetable oil
2 garlic cloves, peeled and finely chopped
2 sirloin steaks, trimmed and sliced thinly
2.5 cm (1 inch) piece of ginger, peeled and finely chopped
4 sticks of lemon grass
1 dessertspoon finely sliced chillies, or to taste

5 tablespoons coconut cream (available in tins)
150 ml (5 fl oz) chicken stock
1 tablespoon soy sauce
1 tablespoon Thai fish sauce
bunch of fresh coriander
4 spring onions, finely sliced

METHOD: Heat 3 tablespoons of oil in a wok and add the garlic, fry until just golden. Add the beef, followed by the ginger, and stir well. Cut the lemon grass lengthways with a sharp knife, ease out the tender central core and chop. Add this to the beef along with the chillies and stir. Then add the coconut cream, stock, soy sauce and fish sauce. Simmer for about 2 minutes, or until the beef is tender.

Stir in a tablespoon of freshly chopped coriander, sprinkle over the spring onions and serve with rice or noodles.

BEEF AND MUSHROOM STIR FRY
WITH GARLIC, BLACK BEANS
AND GINGER

Salted black beans were a welcome discovery for me. Widely used in Chinese cookery, they impart a sweet and sour, almost yeasty flavour to dishes. Cans are the most convenient way of buying them, but you can also buy the cheaper packets from ethnic supermarkets. They are quite salty, so a few go a long way, but they keep for ages in the fridge when transferred to a covered bowl.

SERVES 4

oil for frying
2 garlic cloves, peeled and chopped
2.5 cm (1 inch) piece of ginger, peeled and finely chopped
450 g (1 lb) tail-end fillet of beef
2 carrots, peeled and cut into julienne strips
225 g (½ lb) large flat mushrooms, sliced

2 leeks, trimmed and sliced lengthways
2 fresh chillies, finely chopped
1 head Chinese cabbage, cut into shreds
1 tablespoon salted black beans, roughly mashed
soy sauce

METHOD: Heat 3 tablespoons of oil in a wok or large frying pan. Add the garlic and ginger and fry until golden. Add the meat, which should be thinly sliced, and toss in the hot oil until brown. Add the carrots, mushrooms, leeks and chillies (optional) and continue tossing in the oil for 3 minutes.

Add the Chinese leaves, black beans and a generous dash of soy sauce. Cook for 2 more minutes, check seasoning and serve with rice or noodles.

BEEF AND STOUT STEW
WITH GARLIC MASH

I wasn't quite brought up on Guinness, but coming from Ireland it's almost true. This is more than just the national drink, it's a way of life. Order a pint of Guinness in an Irish pub and it can take quite a few minutes to pour: enough time to discuss the weather, check that your respective families are in good health and pick up on the local gossip. The draught Guinness sold in cans may not have the added ritual, but it is a remarkably good approximation of the real thing.

SERVES 4

olive oil
450 g (1 lb) stewing beef, cubed
2 onions, peeled and chopped
1 head of garlic
4 carrots, peeled and cut into 5 cm (2 inch) strips
2 leeks, trimmed and cut into rounds
4 sticks celery

275 ml (½ pint) Guinness
275 ml (½ pint) beef stock
zest and juice of 1 orange
1 bay leaf
salt and pepper
700 g (1½ lb) potatoes
175 ml (½ pint) milk
2 tablespoons chopped parsley

METHOD: Heat 3 tablespoons of oil in a large casserole dish and brown the meat in batches. Add the onions and sauté, without colouring, for 10 minutes. Add two cloves of the garlic, peeled and finely chopped, along with the carrots, leeks and celery and continue cooking for 5 minutes. Pour in the Guinness and stock, and add the orange zest and bay leaf. Season with salt and pepper, cover and simmer for 1 hour over a low heat.

Peel the remaining garlic cloves and blanch in boiling water for 1 minute, refresh under cold water and pat dry. Heat 5 tablespoons of olive oil in a small saucepan, add the garlic, cover and stew over a gentle heat for 5 minutes, or until the garlic is soft. Mash the garlic and oil together to form a paste. Boil the potatoes until tender, mash, and stir in the garlic along with sufficient warm milk to form the correct consistency. Season with salt and pepper.

Stir the chopped parsley into the stew, check seasoning and serve with the garlic mash.

Meatballs, mash and gremolada

Meatballs were one of the first things I learned to cook. Every time I make them I remember the sound of my mother's wedding ring clicking against the teaspoon as she quickly turned out four meatballs to my one. Hers also seemed so perfectly round and similar in size. But then as she points out I was only five years old and spent rather too much time depositing the contents on my lap. They take a bit of time to prepare, but are well worth it and taste even better the next day.

SERVES 4

450 g (1 lb) minced beef
1 onion, finely chopped
4 garlic cloves, peeled and very finely chopped
2 slices of bread, briefly soaked in milk and squeezed
1 egg
salt and pepper
bunch of fresh thyme
flour

oil
1 glass white wine
1 × 400 g (14 oz) tin of chopped tomatoes
1 tablespoon tomato purée
900 g (2 lb) cooked potatoes
milk
bunch of parsley
2 lemons
bunch of fresh basil

METHOD: Combine the beef, onion, half the garlic, the bread, egg, a generous seasoning of salt and pepper and a generous quantity of thyme in a bowl. Mix well and with a teaspoon, mould balls of the mixture into the palm of your hand. Roll the balls lightly in flour and briefly fry in the oil until lightly brown. Remove the meatballs from the pan.

Pour the oil from the pan and deglaze with the white wine. Stir in the chopped tomatoes, purée and meatballs and cook, covered, over a moderate heat for 40 minutes.

Mash the potatoes and in a saucepan heat 5 tablespoons of olive oil and 175 ml (6 fl oz) of milk. Whisk in the cold potato, adding more milk as you go until you reach the desired consistency. Season with salt and pepper. You can keep this warm in the oven sitting in a roasting tin of boiling water if required.

Chop the remaining garlic and a generous handful of parsley together with the zest from the lemons. Roughly chop the basil. Just before serving, stir the basil into the tomato sauce, pour the meatballs and sauce over the mash and sprinkle over some of the gremolada.

TOULOUSE SAUSAGES WITH CELERIAC PURÉE AND BRAISED SHALLOTS

As a nation we are increasingly rejecting offal, but our appetite for sausages continues to rise. Every butcher has his own recipe which will never be based on prime cuts of meat. Instead, in will go all the flavoursome parts that are either too small or too unsightly to cook, plus some seasoning, and there you have the great British banger in its various forms. The Toulouse sausage is traditionally about 4 cm (1½ inches) in diameter and made of coarsely minced pork.

SERVES 4

1 head of celeriac
salt and pepper
1 onion, peeled and quartered
4 cloves
olive oil

milk
8 Toulouse sausages
450 g (1 lb) shallots, peeled
275 ml (½ pint) cider

METHOD: Peel the celeriac and roughly chop into 2-inch chunks. Add to a saucepan of boiling salted water along with the onion, studded with the cloves. Cook until tender, drain, remove the onion and liquidise the celeriac. Beat in 5 tablespoons of olive oil and enough milk to form the desired consistency, about 150 ml (5 fl oz). Set aside and keep warm.

Fry the sausages in a little oil until cooked through and keep warm. Put the shallots in the same pan, coat thoroughly in oil, cover with tin foil, lower the heat and cook until tender, about 5 minutes. Remove and keep warm.

Drain any excess oil from the pan, add the cider and reduce, scraping up any bits from the bottom of the pan until the liquid becomes a syrup. Serve on top of the sausages with the celeriac purée and shallots.

If you are keeping the purée warm – this goes for mash, too – sit it in a bain marie (a roasting tin half full of boiling water) in a low oven. It will stay happy like this for at least 1 hour.

ITALIAN SAUSAGES WITH WILTED GREENS, WHOLE GARLIC AND THYME

Italian sausages come in many different forms, from the mild corda de Monscia of Lombardy to the chilli-hot versions of the south. Coarsely minced and flavoured with anything from salt and pepper to chilli and fennel seeds, they are one of the staples of that country's peasant food and all the better for being that. Strong sausages are more suitable for this recipe than the milder versions, but buy what you like most. It is also good made with Spanish chorizo, but obviously much stronger in taste.

SERVES 4

450 g (1 lb) spring greens (cabbage or sprouting broccoli)
1 head garlic, split into cloves and peeled
olive oil
8 sausages (about 450 g/1 lb)

1 glass white wine
salt and pepper
1 dessertspoon roughly chopped fresh thyme
Parmesan

METHOD: Heat a large pot of salted water and when boiling add the spring greens, bring back to the boil and cook for 2 minutes. Remove and refresh under cold water. Add the garlic to the water, return to the boil and simmer for 1 minute. Drain and similarly refresh.

Heat 3 tablespoons of olive oil and sauté the sausages until almost cooked. Add the greens and garlic and coat well in the oil. Cover loosely and cook, stirring occasionally, for 5 minutes. Remove the lid, add the white wine, season with salt and pepper and continue cooking uncovered for a further 5 minutes. Stir in the thyme and serve with shavings of Parmesan sprinkled on top.

CUMBERLAND SAUSAGES WITH RED ONION GRAVY, BEETROOT SALAD AND HORSERADISH MASH

It is now possible to buy grated horseradish in jars, not to be confused with the usually repulsive horseradish sauce, which is over-vinegared and full of nasty extra ingredients of dubious distinction. Short of having horseradish in your garden, and someone to dig it up for you, I can think of no better way of procuring this powerful and much underused root.

SERVES 4

8 Cumberland sausages
oil for frying
1 red onion, peeled and chopped
225 ml (8 fl oz) red wine
175 ml (6 fl oz) chicken stock
3 raw beetroot, peeled and roughly
* grated*

salt and pepper
olive oil
275 ml (½ pint) milk
450 g (1 lb) potatoes, cooked, peeled
* and mashed*
2 tablespoons grated horseradish

METHOD: Fry the sausages in a well-oiled frying pan until cooked. Remove and keep warm. Add a little more oil to the pan and fry the red onion for 5 minutes over a moderate heat. Add the red wine and stock and simmer until reduced to a quarter of its original volume.

Season the beetroot with salt and pepper and toss in 2–3 tablespoons of olive oil. Heat the milk and 75 ml (3 fl oz) of olive oil in a saucepan. Beat the potato mixture into the oil and milk and season with salt and pepper.

When you are ready to serve the sausage, add the horseradish to the mash, but don't do this too early, as the heat from the potato gradually lessens the power of the horseradish. Spoon a little of the gravy round the side and serve with the beetroot salad.

Mashed potato can be made with cold potatoes. Cook them the day before with the skins on, for more flavour, then peel them the next day when they are cold.

CHORIZO AND WHITE BEAN STEW

If I had to select one favourite culinary treat from each country, my choice for Spain would be chorizo, although Serrano ham would follow closely. This sausage of pork, paprika, spices, herbs and garlic is delicious eaten as an appetiser, but also has a way of imparting its flavour to other ingredients which is almost magical.

SERVES 4

450 g (1 lb) white beans (e.g. haricot)
110 g (4 oz) pork belly, cut into
 bite-sized pieces
570 ml (1 pint) chicken stock
2 red onions
4 carrots, peeled and cut into batons
olive oil

2 garlic cloves, peeled and finely
 chopped
225 g (½ lb) chorizo, cut into
 bite-sized pieces
salt and pepper
parsley

METHOD: Soak the beans overnight in plenty of water, changing the water 2 or 3 times if possible. Add the drained beans and pork belly to the stock, bring to the boil and simmer for 40 minutes, or until the beans are tender.

Peel and cut the red onion into half-moon slices and sauté along with the carrots in 5 tablespoons of olive oil for 10 minutes without colouring. When the beans and pork belly are just cooked, add to the red onion along with the garlic, chorizo and a seasoning of salt and pepper. Continue cooking for a further 20–30 minutes, or until the chorizo is cooked. Remove 2 cups of the beans and push through a sieve, returning them to the stew. Season with salt and pepper and serve with a generous sprinkling of parsley.

BRAISED VENISON WITH ROOT VEGETABLES AND BLACK SAUCE

Hesitancy about venison usually focuses on dryness and toughness, problems that are inherent in eating the meat from a wild animal. I have had some wonderful examples of wild venison, but if you want consistency it is hard not to be persuaded about the benefits of farmed venison, itself almost a bit of a misnomer – these animals are generally free to wander in fairly large enclosed areas and are usually fed on healthy supplies of carrots and potatoes.

SERVES 4

450 g (1 lb) rump of venison
olive oil
salt and pepper
*4 carrots, peeled and cut into rough
  chunks*
*4 turnips, peeled and cut into rough
  chunks*

*4 parsnips, peeled and cut into rough
  chunks*
12 button onions, peeled
1 glass port
2 tablespoons cassis
5 cm (2 inch) stick of cinnamon

METHOD: Preheat the oven to gas mark 6/400°F/200°C.

Brush the meat with olive oil, season with salt and pepper and fry for about 2 minutes each side. Transfer to the oven and roast for 25–35 minutes.

Blanch the carrots, turnips and parsnips in boiling water for 2 minutes and refresh under cold water. When the meat is cooked, remove to a plate and leave in the switched off oven. Add the root vegetables and button onions to the pan and cook over a moderate heat, covered, until the vegetables are done. You may need a little more oil.

Remove the vegetables from the pan and keep warm. Add the port, cassis and cinnamon. Reduce over a moderate heat for 5 minutes, remove the cinnamon and serve with the vegetables and the meat.

VENISON RAGOUT WITH
OVEN-BAKED POLENTA

Polenta, the earthy yellow Italian purée of maize is normally cooked on top of the stove. For the traditional method see the recipe for braised chicken on page 129. You can also bake it to produce a firmer-textured result, which is a cost-effective alternative when you are already using the oven, as in this recipe. Polenta holds a central place in Italian society and I have visions of gatherings taking place around huge pots of this bubbling yellow fudge.

SERVES 4

700 g (1½ lb) stewing venison, cubed
570 ml (1 pint) red wine
4 carrots, peeled and cut into 5 cm (2 inch) wedges
4 sticks celery, trimmed and cut into 5 cm (2 inch) lengths
2 red onions, peeled and quartered

2 garlic cloves, peeled and finely chopped
2 bay leaves
110 ml (4 fl oz) port
olive oil
salt and pepper
plain flour
275 g (10 oz) polenta

METHOD: Combine the venison, wine, carrots, celery, onions, garlic, bay leaves, port, 5 tablespoons of olive oil and a generous seasoning of pepper in a bowl. Cover and set aside in the fridge overnight; better if it is a few days.

Preheat the oven to gas mark 5/375°F/190°C.

Remove the meat from the marinade, pat dry and toss in seasoned flour, then fry in olive oil until lightly coloured. Remove and put into a casserole. Add the drained vegetables to the frying pan, along with a little extra olive oil if required, and sauté for 5 minutes. Add the vegetables to the meat in the casserole. Pour the marinade into the pan, scraping up any bits sticking to the bottom. Bring to the boil, skim off any froth and pour the marinade over the meat and vegetables. Season with salt and pepper and cook in the oven for 1 hour, covered, or until tender.

Bring 3 pints of water to the boil with 2 teaspoons of salt. Add the polenta in a steady stream, stirring all the time, and then pour into a roasting tin. Put into the oven along with the venison and cook for one hour.

Remove the polenta from the oven and leave in a warm place. Remove the meat from the casserole and reduce the sauce over a high heat for 15 minutes. Liquidise and push through a sieve. Replace the meat and reheat gently before serving with the polenta.

You can omit this last stage if you prefer a more rustic stew, but the sauce will not be quite as thick or rich.

SPICED CHICKEN LIVERS WITH
POPPADOMS AND SALAD

I once spent a year living in India and the high point of the day was the evening visit to the market. When the sun went down and the temperature was supposed to drop a few degrees, I would wander from stall to stall buying the most wonderful vegetables and fruit. Chicken was surprisingly expensive, but this wasn't ordinary chicken. Barns cost too much money to the average Indian farmer, and Indian chickens do what chickens are supposed to do: grub around and hunt for food. I have yet to eat chicken like it.

SERVES 4

225 g (½ lb) button mushrooms, cut
    into quarters
½ teaspoon turmeric
vegetable oil
1 teaspoon cumin seeds
1 small onion, peeled and finely chopped
450 g (1 lb) chicken livers, cleaned
bunch of fresh coriander
ground cumin
1 teaspoon coriander seeds, roughly
    crushed

1 teaspoon ground coriander
2.5 cm (1 inch) piece of fresh ginger,
    peeled and chopped
cayenne pepper
2 tomatoes
1 packet poppadoms
various salad leaves
olive oil
salt

METHOD: Blanch the mushrooms, with the turmeric, in boiling water for 2 minutes. Drain and refresh under cold water and set aside. Heat 3 table-spoons of vegetable oil in a wok and when hot add the cumin seeds. Fry for 1 minute before adding the onion. Continue to cook for 2 minutes, stirring all the time. Add the reserved mushrooms, the chicken livers, 1 dessert-spoon of finely chopped coriander, 1 teaspoon of ground cumin, the coriander seeds and ground coriander, ginger and a pinch of cayenne pepper. Stirring continuously, fry this mixture for 5 minutes, adding a few tablespoons of water if it looks like catching at any time.

Deseed and roughly chop the tomatoes and add to the chicken livers just before serving, along with a generous sprinkling of chopped fresh corian-der. Lightly fry the poppadoms in oil until crisp and drain on kitchen paper. Lightly dress the salad leaves with olive oil. Put a poppadom on each plate and add a generous bunch of salad leaves. Top with the chicken livers, season with salt, and serve.

LAMB'S KIDNEY SAUCE WITH
BUTTERED NOODLES

We used to devour vast quantities of offal in this country and with good reason: it is easy food to prepare and is packed with flavour and vitamins. Lamb's kidneys are one of my favourites – delicate, yet rich; sweet, but with a clean, well-focused flavour and a velvety, smooth texture. Served on top of a mound of buttered noodles, or with some sweet basmati rice, this is a near-instant supper.

SERVES 4

12 lamb's kidneys	*1 glass white wine*
4 tomatoes, deseeded and chopped	*1 dessertspoon each of chopped*
olive oil	*parsley, thyme and tarragon*
2 tablespoons chopped shallots	*50 g (2 oz) butter, cubed*
salt and pepper	*450 g (1 lb) spaghetti or noodles*

METHOD: Remove the skin and fat from the kidneys, cut out the gristly core, roughly chop and set aside. Peel, deseed and roughly chop the tomatoes and set aside. Heat 2 tablespoons of olive oil in a frying pan and sauté the shallots for 5 minutes, without colouring. Add the kidneys, coat well in the oil and sauté over a gentle heat for 2 minutes to take the colour from the meat. Season with salt and pepper and pour in the white wine. Let this bubble and reduce until the kidneys are cooked, about 3 minutes.

Stir in the herbs and tomatoes, remove from the heat and whisk in the butter one cube at a time. Serve with spaghetti or rice dressed with a little more butter. I generally find Parmesan is too strong for this already full-flavoured dish, but some people do like it.

LAMB'S LIVER WITH
SWEET AND SOUR BEETROOT

Lamb's liver may not have the kudos of calf's, but it is a fraction of the price and has a subtle flavour all of its own. As does beetroot, a much overlooked vegetable that I almost prefer eating raw, with its distinctive, rich colour and crunchy, earthy flavour. The leaves, if they are still attached, provide the basis for a delicious soup or, sautéed like spinach, make a wonderful side vegetable. In this recipe the liver's softness is contrasted with the crunch of raw beetroot.

SERVES 4

700 g (1½ lb) lamb's liver
275 ml (½ pint) milk
4 beetroot (about the size of a tennis ball)
5 tablespoons fresh lime juice
5 tablespoons soy sauce
5 tablespoons olive oil
1 teaspoon finely grated fresh ginger
50 g (2 oz) butter
salt and pepper

METHOD: Soak the liver in the milk for 30 minutes, drain and pat dry. Slice the beetroot on a mandolin or with a vegetable peeler. Combine the lime juice, soy sauce, olive oil and ginger. Mix well and set aside for 10 minutes before combining with the beetroot.

Heat the butter in a frying pan and when it is frothing, slide in the liver. Sauté the liver over a gentle heat, so the butter doesn't burn, for 3 minutes each side. Serve with the beetroot and a seasoning of salt and pepper.

CALF'S LIVER WITH BLACK OLIVES, CAPERS AND ROSEMARY

It is tempting, but rarely rewarding, to reach for a jar of capers from the supermarket shelves. Steeped in vinegar, the sensation is sharp and rather short. Where is the flavour of the caper? In most cases, lost in the industrial process designed, not to preserve the berry's flavour, but to get it into that jar as efficiently as possible. Try some of the Italian brands, particularly the salted versions, and you will see what I mean. A rescue remedy for the over-vinegared is to wash and gently squeeze them in several changes of cold water.

SERVES 4

110 g (4 oz) black olives, destoned and   *salt and pepper*
   roughly chopped   *balsamic vinegar*
1 tablespoon capers   *4 generous slices of calf's liver*
1 teaspoon finely chopped rosemary   *1 glass red wine*
olive oil

METHOD: Combine the black olives, capers, rosemary and 5 tablespoons of olive oil. Season with salt and pepper and add 1 teaspoon of balsamic vinegar.

Lightly oil a frying pan and sauté the liver for barely 1 minute each side. Remove from the pan to 4 warm plates and season with salt and pepper.

Pour off any excess oil, return the pan to the heat and deglaze with the glass of red wine and 5 tablespoons of balsamic vinegar. Season the wine with salt and pepper and when reduced by half, pour over the liver. Serve with a little of the caper and olive mixture on top.

POTATO SOUFFLÉS WITH CALF'S LIVER AND BUTTERED SAGE

There is a lot of fuss made over soufflés which, unfortunately, seems to discourage people from cooking them. The gentle closing of oven doors and whispering is really not necessary; they are far more robust than is popularly imagined. Their greatest advantage, in my view, is that once they are in the oven you know exactly how long it will be before you eat, which makes anticipation all the more enjoyable and timing the rest of the food all the easier.

SERVES 4

225 g (½ lb) cooked potatoes
3 eggs, separated
5 tablespoons single cream
salt and pepper

50 g (2 oz) butter
2 tablespoons breadcrumbs
4 slices of calf's liver
1 tablespoon sage leaves

METHOD: Mash the potato and mix with the egg yolks, cream and a seasoning of salt and pepper. Be generous with the latter. It is easy to underseason a soufflé – remember all that increase in volume. This can all be done in advance.

Preheat the oven to gas mark 6/400°F/200°C.

At the last minute, whisk the egg whites stiffly and fold the potato mixture in gently. Lightly butter a soufflé dish and dust with the breadcrumbs. Spoon the mixture in gently and bake for 20 minutes.

Melt the remaining butter in a frying pan and sauté the liver for 1 minute each side, adding the sage leaves for the final minute. Serve with generous spoonfuls of the soufflé.

STEAMED BLACK PUDDING WITH
CHERRY TOMATO AND
MUSTARD-SEED SALAD

The first time I ever dry-fried mustard seeds I ended up with the entire contents of the pan on the floor. These are lively pods, and heat makes them extremely active, so have a lid or some tin foil nearby. I normally eat this as a light supper dish, but with a few potatoes and broccoli it becomes more substantial. The pudding is rich, so a little goes a long way.

SERVES 4

450–700g (1–1½ lb) black pudding, depending on greed
450 g (1 lb) cherry tomatoes
bunch of spring onions, trimmed and chopped
olive oil

1 tablespoon black mustard seeds
salt and pepper
1 red or yellow pepper, deseeded and finely chopped
pinch of cayenne pepper

METHOD: Roll the black pudding lightly in tin foil, place in the top of a steamer and cook for 15 minutes. Roughly chop the cherry tomatoes and mix with the spring onions and 75 ml (3 fl oz) of olive oil. Heat a dry frying pan and add the mustard seeds. Cover with a lid or tin foil and fry for about 30 seconds. Add to the tomatoes along with a seasoning of salt and pepper, the red or yellow pepper and a pinch of cayenne pepper.

Remove the black pudding from the steamer and unwrap. Cut diagonally into 1 cm (½ inch) thick slices and serve with the tomato salad.

Desserts

It may be slices of tart, the melting softness of cheesecake or the sublime delights of crisp filo pastry – whatever your weakness for desserts is, the wickedness of indulgence seems part of the delight. Fashion dictates that while in almost every other area of cooking we race round the world in search of new tastes and sensations, when it comes to desserts we remain firmly in this country, or occasionally in France. Witness the return of such nursery favourites as bread and butter pudding, crumbles and pies, charlottes and rice puddings for the colder months; summer pudding, soft fruit and ices for the warmer ones.

In my house, puddings consists of fruit and cheese most of the time, but these recipes are the ones I use when a proper desert is called for. None of them takes much time. They are designed to fit in after the main course has been done and hopefully to be bubbling away on top of the stove or in the oven while everyone is eating.

For the tarts by all means use frozen pastry if you need to save time, but there are one or two essentials. Always use a metal flan tin with removable base (with ceramic flan dishes the pastry melts before it cooks). Roll the pastry directly on to the base and then lift it into the ring – that way you handle it less. Refrigerate at this stage for half an hour (I usually pop it in the freezer for 10 minutes) and then put straight into the oven on to a baking sheet. The latter item of equipment is important to make the pastry crisp.

HONEY AND ALMOND TART

The bees we see in summer may appear to be buzzing about aimlessly, but nothing could be further from the truth. Seventy years ago Nobel-prize winner Karl von Frisch showed how a bee will dance and shake its body in order to tell other bees where the best nectar is. Off they fly, sometimes up to three miles away, for the choice liquid. No wonder there is so much buzzing – it must be quite a mouthful to explain to your colleagues that the flower bed 25 gardens down on the left-hand side is full of raspberries (a fruit renowned in the bee kingdom for its high nectar content). The combination of honey and almonds make this a tart to cheer the cold winter months.

SERVES 6

225 g (8 oz) frozen shortcrust pastry, defrosted	3 eggs
	50 g (2 oz) butter, melted
175 g (6 oz) roasted flaked almonds	2 tablespoons amaretto di Saronno
6 tablespoons honey	6 tablespoons crème fraîche

METHOD: Preheat the oven to gas mark 4/350°F/180°C.

Roll the pastry out and line a 23 cm (9 inch) tart tin, pressing the pastry lightly into the sides. Refrigerate for half an hour and then bake for 30 minutes. Meanwhile briefly blitz the almonds in a liquidiser or food processor and combine with the honey, eggs, butter and amaretto.

Pour the mixture into the tart case and bake for a further 20 minutes, or until the mixture has just set. Remove to a wire rack and allow to cool. Serve at room temperature with the crème fraîche.

ALMOND BISCUITS

If I lived in France I doubt I would make tarts – too easy and delicious to buy them locally. We may not have the same standard of tart-making in this country, but when it comes to ice-cream we seem to have become an equal match for the Italians, who, I think, have some of the best ice-cream in the world. It's a near-instant dessert, and easily dressed up with these biscuits, which don't take long to make.

MAKES ABOUT 30

110 g (4 oz) plain flour	50 g (2 oz) sugar
110 g (4 oz) ground almonds	50 g (2 oz) flaked almonds
pinch of salt	1 egg, separated
175 g (6 oz) butter	few drops of extract of vanilla

METHOD: Sieve the flour and mix with the ground almonds and a pinch of salt. Rub the butter in with your fingertips and add the sugar and almost all the flaked almonds. Beat in the egg yolk and vanilla extract and roll into a long tube. Wrap in cling film and refrigerate for 1 hour.

Preheat the oven to gas mark 4/350°F/180°C.

Cut ½ cm (¼ inch) slices from the length of pastry and arrange on a baking tray, leaving a little room round the edge for the biscuits to expand. Paint each biscuit with the egg white and press a few remaining flaked almonds into the biscuits. Bake until the biscuits are golden, about 20 minutes. Remove to a wire tray and allow to cool.

I usually do two or three batches of these biscuits when I make them. Partnered with ice-cream and chocolate sauce they make a delicious dessert that has got me out of more than one or two tight corners.

SPICED APPLE CRUSTARDS

Filo pastry produces wonderfully golden crispy results – packaging of the best kind. Keep the pastry moist and work as quickly as possible and you should have no problem. This is a good dish to do because it's better if things don't go too smoothly. You want air pockets and rough edges, crumpled paper rather than a well-made bed look. You will need 4 shallow metal tart tins about 10 cm (4 inches) in diameter.

SERVES 4

8 Cox's orange pippin apples	*cinnamon*
275 g (10 oz) sugar	*nutmeg*
250 g (9 oz) butter	*ground cloves*
packet of filo pastry	*150 ml (5 fl oz) cream*

METHOD: Preheat the oven to gas mark 4/350°F/180°C and lightly butter the tart tins. Peel, quarter and core the apples. In a wide, shallow frying pan heat the sugar and 150 g (5 oz) of the butter together at a fairly high temperature so it caramelises, but don't let it burn. Allow to cook for 2 or 3 minutes until it gets a nice even colour.

Add the apples and continue to cook until covered in the caramel – about 6 minutes. Use a wooden spoon to coat the apples with the mixture.

Melt the remaining butter and dampen two tea towels – these are to keep the pastry moist. Unroll the packet of filo and tear the first sheet into strips across the length about 7.5 cm (3 inches) wide. Arrange like the spokes of a wheel around the first of the tart tins, brushing with melted butter as you go. Keep the remaining pastry covered with the damp cloth. You may need more than one sheet; the aim is to have a solid circle of pastry surrounding the tin.

Place a dollop of the apples and sauce in the middle of the pastry and sprinkle over a little of the spices. Keep back a small amount of the caramel for the final sauce. Fold each spoke of the filo into the middle, coating each one liberally with the melted butter and trying to build up as many air pockets and folds as possible. Tear up another sheet and build up a cone shape on top, using plenty of butter, with as many folds as you can. Repeat for the other 3 tart tins and bake in the oven for 30 minutes, or until brown.

For the final sauce, reheat the remains of the apple caramel, stir in the cream and serve with the crustards.

BANANA BURNT CREAM

Burnt cream is thought to have originated in Cambridge and there is much argument as to whether it predates or follows the more famous *crème brûlée*. In a spirit of Anglo-French cooperation, I venture to suggest it probably goes to show the cross-development of both cuisines, more than anything else.

SERVES 6

1 vanilla pod, or a few drops of
*   vanilla essence*
570 ml (1 pint) full cream milk
6 egg yolks

50 g (2 oz) caster sugar
2 bananas, peeled and cut into ½ cm
*   (¼ inch) discs*
soft brown sugar

METHOD: Preheat the oven to gas mark 4/350°F/180°C.

Run the point of a knife down the vanilla pod, then hold the pod over a saucepan and run your thumbnail down its length. Drop both the seeds that come out and the pod into the saucepan and add the milk (you can also add a few drops of vanilla essence if you want to increase the vanilla taste further).

Bring the milk to the boil and simmer gently for 1 minute exactly. Beat the egg yolks thoroughly with the caster sugar until they take on a pale colour. Remove the milk from the heat and pour on to the eggs, whisking all the time. Pour the mixture into a shallow gratin dish with the banana in the bottom and place in a roasting tin half filled with boiling water. Bake for 25 minutes, or until set. Cool and refrigerate.

When you are ready to serve, cover with soft brown sugar as evenly as possible. Place the dish under a preheated grill until the sugar melts, remove, allow to cool so it crisps up and serve.

You can also do this in individual ramekins, in which case they should only take 15–20 minutes to set in the oven.

BLACKBERRY TART

I can't help but resent paying for blackberries. Neat punnets in supermarkets seem so incongruous for this typically wild and untamed fruit. Surely part of the joy is in the picking – stretching out for that particularly black and apparently juice-laden berry that is infuriatingly out of reach. Blackberries seem to thrive in poor soil, the fruit somehow sitting oddly on those inhospitable brambles. Not as refined as raspberries maybe, but with an honest intensity that is almost sinful. A lush, dark, ripe, juicy blackberry is a delight; I somehow can't believe that something so small and uncultivated can taste so wonderful.

SERVES 6

225 g (8 oz) shortcrust pastry
275 g (10 oz) blackberries
110 g (4 oz) caster sugar
3 eggs

110 g (4 oz) unsalted butter, melted
juice of 1 lemon
2 tablespoons cassis

METHOD: Preheat the oven to gas mark 2/300°F/150°C.

Roll out the pastry and line a 23 cm (9 inch) tart tin. Prick with a fork and bake in the oven for 30 minutes. Remove and allow to cool.

Gently stew the blackberries with the sugar until soft, about 5 minutes. Push the cooked blackberries through a sieve into a bowl. Whisk in the eggs, the melted butter, lemon juice and cassis and pour into the pastry case. Bake in the oven for 20–25 minutes, or until set. Serve at room temperature.

BREAD AND BUTTER PUDDING

Part of the excitement about British food at the moment is the way in which old-fashioned puddings have returned and sit quite happily alongside newcomers. One of my favourites is bread and butter pudding, but made with the Italian panettone instead of the more usual plain bread, which gives it a richer quality.

SERVES 6

1 glass brandy
225 g (½ lb) prunes
cold tea
6 slices of panettone pudding
unsalted butter

2 strips of lemon peel
225 ml (8 fl oz) milk
225 ml (8 fl oz) double cream
4 egg yolks
50 g (2 oz) caster sugar

METHOD: Heat the brandy, set alight, allow to flame and then cool. Soak the prunes for a couple of hours in tea, remove the stones and add to the brandy. Butter a pie dish and starting with a layer of panettone arrange a scattering of prunes, then more panettone and so on, finishing up with panettone – the slices should come about two thirds up the side of the dish.

Preheat the oven to gas mark 4/350°F/180°C.

Put the lemon peel, milk and cream in a saucepan and bring to the boil, removing the saucepan from the heat just before it reaches boiling point. Combine the egg yolks with the caster sugar and beat until pale.

Pour the hot milk and cream mixture over the eggs, stirring all the time. Pour into the pie dish and place the dish in a roasting tin. Add boiling water to the roasting tin until two thirds up the sides and bake for 25 minutes, or until set.

DAMSON AND CINNAMON CRUMBLE

Damsons are with us in the autumn, an old-fashioned fruit that often gets overlooked because it is only with us for a short time. For my money this makes it more of an exotic ingredient, along with chestnuts and sprouting broccoli than, say, asparagus (with us all year now), kiwi fruit and mangoes. Peeling damsons does take a bit of time and one short-cut is to combine them with plums if speed is necessary. Otherwise go the whole hog – pour yourself a glass of wine and turn on the radio. Damsons do stain your hands, so you might like to consider wearing a pair of gloves.

SERVES 4

900 g (2 lb) damsons
275 g (10 oz) caster sugar
cinnamon
25 g (1 oz) flour

50 g (2 oz) dark brown sugar
50 g (2 oz) ground hazelnuts
50 g (2 oz) butter

METHOD: Preheat the oven to gas mark 4/350°F/180°C.

Stone the damsons and place in a deep, ovenproof pie dish with 2 tablespoons of water and the caster sugar. Sprinkle over a generous pinch of cinnamon.

Combine the flour, dark brown sugar and hazelnuts and work in the butter. Spread over the damsons and bake for 35 minutes.

Fried Bread and Honey

When I first ate this dish in Spain it was under a bright November sky. Lunch had gone on for hours and this was the final stroke of genius. We all waxed lyrical about the quality of the bread and how crucial it must be to the dish. Imagine our horror when, summoned, the cook explained she had run out of bread and had sent her son to the local shop where they had nothing but sliced white to offer. I hate to admit it, but I almost think that, in this case, the worse the quality of bread, the better the dish.

SERVES 4

175 ml (6 fl oz) white wine
pinch of nutmeg
pinch of cinnamon
pinch of ground cloves
25 g (1 oz) caster sugar

2 eggs
four slices of bread, crusts removed
110 ml (4 fl oz) olive oil
4 dessertspoons honey

METHOD: Put the wine in a shallow bowl with the nutmeg, cinnamon, cloves and sugar and mix together. Lightly beat the eggs in a separate bowl. Dip both sides of the bread in the wine and then in the egg. Heat the oil in a deep saucepan and when sufficiently hot – drop a bit of egg in to see if it cooks – fry the bread slices until they are brown on both sides. You will need to turn them over during the cooking. Drain on kitchen paper to get rid of the excess oil.

In a small saucepan heat the honey with 4 dessertspoons of water, stirring all the time until it reaches a runny consistency. Pour over the bread and serve.

GRILLED PANETTONE WITH
MAPLE SYRUP, PECANS
AND CRÈME FRAÎCHE

Panettone, a Christmas cake so light in texture and buttery in taste that it has become a year-round feature, originates in Milan where, the story goes, there lived a baker called Toni. His beautiful daughter was much admired by a local aristocrat who, realising there was little chance of bridging the social gap, offered to come and apprentice himself to Toni. He turned out to be a dab hand at baking and, given his love of good things, started to squeeze more eggs and butter into the dough, along with raisins and candied peel. I give you pan di Toni. This story is told by Anna Del Conte in her excellent and fascinating *Gastronomy of Italy*, just one of her essential books on Italian food and cooking. This dish, more a combination than a recipe, was the result of leftover panettone which I simply couldn't bear to throw out.

SERVES 4

unsalted butter
4 slices of panettone
4 tablespoons maple syrup

50 g (2 oz) pecans
4 tablespoons crème fraîche

METHOD: Lightly butter the panettone and toast under a preheated grill until brown and bubbling. Spoon over the maple syrup and pecans, top with the crème fraîche and serve.

PEACH TARTLETS

The peach is a native of China – is it any wonder that country holds fruit and vegetables in such high esteem? It has journeyed across the world and sprouted over 2,000 varieties, but none to equal the peaches of immortality that fruit every 6,000 years. These trees were feasted on by the gods, who were then able to live for ever, or at least for another 6,000 years before the next peach-eating session.

SERVES 6

225 g (8 oz) puff pastry	*3 eggs*
4 peaches	*50 g (2 oz) caster sugar*
3 tablespoons brandy	*75 g (3 oz) unsalted butter, melted*

METHOD: Preheat the oven to gas mark 4/350°F/180°C.

Roll out the pastry and line six shallow 10 cm (4 inch) tartlet tins. Slice the peaches, removing the stones, toss in the brandy and arrange in the pastry shells.

Whisk the eggs, sugar and melted butter and slowly heat in a saucepan until almost set – you can tell by running your finger along the back of the wooden spoon. Immediately pour into the pastry cases on top of the peaches. Bake in the oven for 15–20 minutes, or until set. Serve at room temperature.

Partly cooking the custard before adding it to the pastry case helps to prevent the pastry going soggy.

PEAR AND AMARETTI CHEESECAKE

The Italians traditionally ate their biscotti in the middle of the morning, with a glass of sweet wine for company, a practice that we would do well to introduce in this country. What a wonderful idea if we could all down tools and sip a glass of something strong and sweet and crunch on biscuits for no particular reason other than sheer indulgence. You can use various types of amaretti for this recipe, but I have found the most successful are the cantucci di Prato, available from most supermarkets and Italian delicatessens. This cheesecake does not contain gelatin, so the top is not set quite so firmly as you would normally expect.

SERVES 4–6

110 g (4 oz) cantucci di Prato
75 g (3 oz) melted butter
4 pears
110 g (4 oz) caster sugar
7.5 cm (3 inch) stick of cinnamon

5 tablespoons brandy
275 g (10 oz) Ricotta
275 ml (10 fl oz) double cream
½ teaspoon ground cinnamon

METHOD: Grind the cantucci di Prato in a food processor or with a rolling pin and mix with the melted butter. Spread the mixture over the base of a 20 cm (8 inch) tart or cake tin with a removable base and refrigerate.

Peel and quarter the pears and put in a saucepan with 50 g (2 oz) of caster sugar, 275 ml (½ pint) of water and the cinnamon stick. Bring to the boil and simmer the fruit for 10 minutes, or until tender. Remove the fruit, add the brandy to the syrup, continue cooking until it reduces and becomes slightly sticky and reserve.

Push the Ricotta through a sieve with a wooden spoon and mix with the double cream and the remaining sugar. Stir in the ground cinnamon. Lay the pears on the biscuit base, cover with the Ricotta and cream, dust with a little more cinnamon and refrigerate for 1 hour. Don't leave it in the fridge for more than a few hours or the base will go soggy. Serve with a little of the syrup on the side.

SPICED PEAR TARTE TATIN

By the seventeenth century pears had become so popular in France they were almost like an aristocratic currency: introducing a new pear at court could lead to the bestowing of all sorts of favours and if Louis XIV was tempted by your offering, your future was secure. Reading about this period of such excitement surrounding fruit and vegetables feels remarkably similar to what is happening today. The court may have become the supermarket, the customer the king and the pears rediscovered rather than invented, but the introduction of 'new' breeds is a welcome feature of modern horticulture. For this dish, choose a firm pear. If it is mushy it is likely to collapse in the cooking.

SERVES 6

caster sugar
700 g (1½ lb) pears, peeled, halved
and cored

½ teaspoon each of cinnamon, ground
cloves and nutmeg
225 g (8 oz) puff pastry

METHOD: Preheat the oven to gas mark 5/375°F/190°C.

Put 110 g (4 oz) of caster sugar in a shallow, ovenproof pan and caramelise over a moderate heat until dark, but not burned – if it burns, you'll need to start again. Remove from the heat, put one pear half, cut-side up, in the middle, arrange the remaining pear halves around it and sprinkle over the spices.

Roll out the pastry and place on top of the pears, tucking the edges in. Bake for 30 minutes, or until brown. Rest for 10 minutes, turn on to a plate and serve – there may be extra juice from the pears, so take care.

PINEAPPLE CAKE

There is something very welcoming about a pineapple, a symbol of hospitality whether real and edible, or made of stone and atop the gateposts of a house. In Scotland, for instance, there is an entire folly complete with rooms in the shape of a pineapple where you can go and stay. Pineapple is a perfect partner for rum and when I'm feeling lazy, I stop proceedings after soaking the two together, grab a fork and settle down. The cake can wait for another day.

SERVES 6

1 pineapple
rum
175 g (6 oz) butter
175 g (6 oz) caster sugar

4 eggs, beaten
175 g (6 oz) self-raising flour
1 teaspoon baking powder

METHOD: Preheat the oven to gas mark 4/350°F/180°C.

Peel, core and slice the pineapple. Lay the slices out in a shallow bowl and sprinkle a generous amount of rum over the fruit. Melt a little extra butter and brush the insides of a shallow ovenproof casserole dish. Sprinkle on a little sugar and distribute evenly.

Cream the butter and sugar together, fold in the eggs and add the flour and baking powder, both sieved.

Lay the pineapple slices out on the bottom of the dish, spoon over the cake mixture and bake in the oven for about 50 minutes or until cooked. Serve with loads of cream and a spoonful of the juice from the soaking.

GRILLED PINK GRAPEFRUIT WITH
SAFFRON AND HONEY CREAM

One November I went on a trip to the plains of La Mancha in Spain to watch saffron, the dried stigmas of *crocus sativus* being picked. Never have I been so cold. I stood watching a family bent double making their way slowly up a field as the wind swept, unbroken, across this flat and open country-side. I tried to help, but after five minutes my back was agony and I couldn't feel my feet or hands. Since then I count out the strands of saffron I use, remembering how much hard work has gone into producing it.

SERVES 4

4 pink grapefruit
4 dessertspoons demerara sugar
275 ml (10 fl oz) single cream

2 dessertspoons honey
generous pinch of saffron

METHOD: Cut each grapefruit in half, scoop out the flesh from both halves and in each case, pile into half so you have 4 half-grapefruits containing all the flesh. Sprinkle over the sugar and set aside.

In a small saucepan heat the cream and honey (if you scoop out the honey using a spoon held under the hot tap the honey will slip off). Sprinkle in the saffron threads and continue to heat until the cream almost comes to the boil. Remove and allow to cool.

Preheat the grill. Grill the grapefruit until brown and bubbling and serve with the saffron and honey cream.

PLUM CHARLOTTES WITH
CINNAMON CREAM

It is a peculiarly British habit to differentiate between plums and gages – most countries consider them the same thing. There are many varieties, although we get to see but a few of these in the shops. There is nothing to beat a good plum, almost translucent in the late summer sunlight, the stone a shadow in the middle and the surface a dusty hue.

SERVES 6

275 g (10 oz) plums
caster sugar
5 tablespoons brandy
10 cm (4 inch) cinnamon stick
275 ml (10 fl oz) single cream

110 g (4 oz) melted butter
6–8 slices of good quality white bread,
crusts removed
6 cloves

METHOD: Stone and roughly dice the plums and place in a bowl. Toss with 75 g (3 oz) of sugar and pour over the brandy. Put the cinnamon and cream into a saucepan, heat almost to boiling point, remove from the heat and allow to infuse.

Meanwhile brush the insides of 6 dariole moulds (or small pudding basins) with melted butter. Put a spoonful of sugar into one and twist it round so the sides are thoroughly coated. Pour any loose sugar into the next mould and continue until you have finished all 6 moulds.

Line each mould with the bread. It doesn't matter if the bread is in pieces, provided you seal the joins well by pressing the bread firmly together. With a pastry cutter, cut out 6 bread lids.

Preheat the oven to gas mark 6/400°F/200°C.

Liberally coat the bread lining with butter, half fill each mould with plums, put a clove in the centre of each one, and fill up with the remaining plums, keeping back the brandy-plum juice. Brush the edges with butter, put the lid on and brush it with butter, too, and sprinkle over a little sugar. Bake in the oven for 30 minutes, or until the tops are brown and crispy.

Simmer the brandy-plum juice down to a syrup. Turn the charlottes on to warm plates and serve with the juice, and lots of the cream, strained of the cinnamon.

POACHED PEACHES WITH
CARDAMOM AND RUM CREAM

Not so long ago our peach season barely stretched from July through to September, a situation now changed with modern methods of transport and distribution but also fraught with frustration. However perfect peaches are to look at, they can be a bitter disappointment to eat, and no amount of poaching, roasting or marinating will help a tough and tasteless peach. I'm told you can grow them outside in this country and with a good summer they will have a rich colour and flavour, although they are unlikely to ripen to the subtle softness of the famous Montreuil. With a good quality peach, gentle poaching will release the flavours fully.

SERVES 4

8 peaches
275 ml (10 fl oz) white wine
50 g (2 oz) sugar

6 cardamom pods
275 ml (10 fl oz) whipping cream
3 tablespoons rum

METHOD: Quarter the peaches and put in a saucepan along with the stones. Pour over the white wine, 275 ml (10 fl oz) of water, the sugar, and cardamom pods. Cover, slowly bring to the boil and simmer for 10 minutes, or until the peaches are tender. Remove the peach quarters and set aside. Bring the syrup to a rolling boil and cook down until it thickens, about 15 minutes. Allow to cool and strain over the peaches, discarding the stones and cardamom pods.

Whip the cream to soft peaks, stir in the rum and serve with the peaches.

RHUBARB BAVAROISE

A well-made bavaroise is a deliciously light dessert and yet full of those lovely pudding ingredients – sugar, cream and fruit purée – a set fool, really. Resistance to gelatin is understandable, as too much can spoil a dish, but handled correctly it should be able to do its job as a setting agent unobtrusively. It is also quite healthy, containing all but one of the essential amino acids and very little fat. What more can you ask for in a dessert laced with cream!

SERVES 4

450 g (1 lb) rhubarb, trimmed and cut into 2.5 cm (1 inch) lengths
110 g (4 oz) sugar
1 vanilla pod

4 leaves of gelatin (10 g/½ oz)
225 ml (8 fl oz) whipping cream
almond oil
50 g (2 oz) roasted almonds

METHOD: Cook the rhubarb with all but a tablespoon of the sugar (you may not need it all) and the vanilla pod. Stew, covered, over a gentle heat for 10 minutes, or until soft. Remove the vanilla (you can keep it in the sugar bowl and use it again) and liquidise. Check for sweetness and add the remaining sugar if required.

Melt the gelatin with 110 ml (4 fl oz) of hot water and whisk the rhubarb into the gelatin. Whip the cream lightly and fold into the rhubarb. Lightly oil a mould or pudding dish with almond oil and pour in the rhubarb mixture. When it is cool, cover with cling film and refrigerate until set, a couple of hours.

To unmould, immerse briefly in hot water if it refuses to come out the first time and invert on to a plate. Sprinkle the almonds on top and serve.

CARAMELISED RICE PUDDINGS
WITH ORANGE SALAD

Why rice pudding should be confined to tins, or the memory of school dinners, I do not understand. It is one of the most sublime puddings. Rich, refreshing and light, it is open to all manner of variations. Try cardamom, cinnamon or nutmeg – all carry the forgotten mystery of Eastern spices. It is easy to imagine how men died in their attempts to race back with boatloads of these culinary gems.

SERVES 4

10 g (½ oz) butter
3 dessertspoons short-grain rice
570 ml (1 pint) milk
1 dessertspoon caster sugar

5 cm (2 inch) cinnamon pod
2 oranges
Cointreau
3 tablespoons demerara sugar

METHOD: Melt the butter in a saucepan, add the rice and coat in the butter. Stir in the milk and the caster sugar. Add the cinnamon and simmer until the rice is tender, about 30 minutes.

Drop the oranges into boiling water for 1 minute, drain and refresh under cold water and peel, making sure to remove as much of the pith as possible. Slice thinly and toss with 3 tablespoons of Cointreau.

Pour the milk and rice into 4 ramekins, reserving the cinnamon pod which can be rinsed in cold water and used again. Allow to cool and refrigerate. Sprinkle demerara sugar over each ramekin and place under a hot grill until the sugar caramelises. Allow to cool and serve with the orange salad.

Blow torches may seem a rather excessive expenditure for this last job, but many professional kitchens use them because they give a lighter, more even crust. If you happen to have one, it's certainly more fun than turning on the grill.

BIBLIOGRAPHY

Allen, Brigid, *Food – An Oxford Anthology*, Oxford University Press, 1994.
Bareham, Lindsey, *In Praise of the Potato*, Michael Joseph, 1989.
　A Celebration of Soup, Michael Joseph, 1993.
Beck, Simone, Bertholle, Louisette and Child, Julia, *Mastering the Art of French Cooking*, Alfred A. Knopf, 1961.
Bell, Annie, *Evergreen*, Bantam, 1994.
Bissell, Frances, *A Cook's Calendar*, Chatto and Windus, 1985.
　The Real Meat Cookbook, Chatto and Windus, 1992.
Boxer, Arabella, *Arabella Boxer's Book of English Food*, Hodder and Stoughton, 1991.
Brown, Lynda, *Fresh Thoughs on Food*, Chatto and Windus, 1986.
Burton-Race, John, *Recipes from an English Master Chef*, Headline, 1994.
Clair, Colin, *Of Herbs and Spices*, Abelard-Schuman, 1961.
Costa, Margaret, *Margaret Costa's Four Seasons Cookery Book*, Thomas Nelson 1970.
David, Elizabeth, *French Country Cooking*, John Lehmann, 1951.
　Italian Food, Macdonald, 1954.
　Summer Cooking, Museum Press, 1955.
　French Provincial Cooking, Michael Joseph, 1960.
　Spices, Salt and Aromatics in the English Kitchen, Penguin Books, 1970.
Davidson, Alan, *North Atlantic Seafood*, Macmillan, 1979.
Del Conte, Anna, *Gastronomy of Italy*, Prentice Hall Press, 1987.
　Secrets from an Italian Kitchen, Bantam Press, 1989.
　Entertaining All'Italiana, Bantam Press, 1991.
Fisher, M.F.K., *The Art of Eating*, Collier Books, 1937.
Grigson, Jane, *Jane Grigson's Fish Book*, International Wine and Food Society, 1973.
　Jane Grigson's Vegetable Book, Michael Joseph, 1978.
　Jane Grigson's Fruit Book, Michael Joseph, 1982.
Grigson, Sophie, *Sophie Grigson's Ingredients Book*, Pyramid, 1991.
Guérard, Michel, *Cuisine Minceur*, Macmillan, 1977.
Hopkinson, Simon, *Roast Chicken and Other Stories*, Ebury, 1994.
Jaffrey, Madhur, *Madhur Jaffrey's Indian Cookery*, BBC Books, 1982.
Jardine-Paterson, Victoria and McKelvie, Colin, *Good Game*, Swan Hill Press, 1993.
Koffmann, Pierre, *Memories of Gascony*, The Octopus Group, 1990.
　La Tante Claire, Headline, 1992.
Little, Alastair, *Keep it Simple*, Conran Octopus, 1993.

Madison, Deborah, *The Savoury Way*, Bantam Press, 1990.

Manjon, Maite, *The Gastronomy of Spain and Portugal*, Prentice Hall Press, 1990.

McGee, Harold, *On Food and Cooking*, Charles Scribner's Sons, 1984.

    The Curious Cook, North Point Press, 1990.

Olney, Richard, *Simple French Food*, Atheneum, 1974.

Ortiz, Elizabeth Lambert, *The Food of Spain and Portugal*, Lennard Publishing, 1989.

Owen, Sri, *The Rice Book*, Doubleday, 1993.

    Indonesian Regional Food and Cookery, Doubleday, 1994.

Rance, Patrick, *The French Cheese Book*, Macmillan, 1989.

Robuchon, Jöel and Wells, Patricia, *Cuisine Actuelle*, Macmillan, 1991.

Roden, Claudia, *Mediterranean Cookery*, BBC Books, 1987.

Root, Waverley, *The Food of France*, Macmillan, 1958.

    The Food of Italy, Atheneum, 1971.

Rosso, Julee and Lukins, Sheila, *The Silver Palate Good Times Cookbook*, Workman Publishing, 1984.

Round, Jeremy, *The Independent Cook*, Barrie and Jenkins, 1988.

Sevilla, María José, *Spain on a Plate*, BBC Books, 1992.

Simon, André, *André Simon's Guide to Good Food and Wine*, Collins 1952.

Spry, Constance and Hume, Rosemary, *The Constance Spry Cookery Book*, Dent, 1956.

Stein, Richard, *English Seafood Cookery*, Penguin, 1988.

Strang, Jeanne, *Goose Fat and Garlic*, Kyle Cathie, 1989.

Taruschio, Ann and Franco, *Leaves from the Walnut Tree*, Pavilion, 1993.

Troisgros, Jean and Pierre, *The Nouvelle Cuisine of Jean and Pierre Troisgros*, Macmillan 1980.

Wolfert, Paul, *Couscous and Other Good Food from Morocco*, Harper and Row, 1973.

INDEX